AF407278

Chapter 1: Introduction

Welcome to "The Adventurous Bride's Guide to Elopement: Embracing the Outdoors"! I'm thrilled to be your companion on this exciting journey into the world of outdoor weddings, tailored for brides who share a love for nature and a passion for adventure.

In this chapter, we'll kick off our exploration by delving into the mindset of the adventurous bride, dissecting what makes the idea of an outdoor elopement so uniquely appealing. As we embark on this guide, it's not just about planning a wedding; it's about crafting an experience that resonates with the essence of who you are and the love you share.

Are you someone who dreams of saying your vows beneath the open sky, surrounded by the beauty of towering trees or the serenity of a mountaintop? If so, you're in the right place. We'll explore the magic of connecting with nature in your wedding celebrations, embracing the idea that your love story deserves a backdrop as extraordinary as the love itself.

As you flip through these pages, you'll discover the joy of choosing an outdoor location that speaks to your heart. We'll navigate the legalities and permits required for your dream setting, ensuring a smooth path to your outdoor oasis. Accessibility and logistics might seem daunting, but fear not! We'll guide you through the practical aspects, making sure your celebration is not only breathtaking but also hassle-free.

Throughout this guide, we'll tackle the ever-changing factor of weather, helping you embrace the elements rather than fear them. Whether you're planning a summer soiree or a winter wonderland, we've got you covered with tips to keep the weather from raining on your parade.

So, grab a cup of your favorite beverage, settle into your coziest chair, and let's embark on this adventure together. The journey begins here, with the promise of a wedding celebration that reflects your love, your style, and the awe-inspiring beauty of the great outdoors. Get ready to turn the page and step into a world where nature becomes the canvas for your love story.

Defining the Adventurous Bride

Meet the adventurous bride – a spirited soul with a heart full of wanderlust and a vision that stretches beyond traditional wedding norms. She's not just planning a ceremony; she's scripting an experience that mirrors her love for the extraordinary. This bride is drawn to the allure of the outdoors, captivated by the idea of exchanging vows beneath the vast expanse of the sky or amidst the whispers of the forest.

So, what defines the adventurous bride? It's not just about seeking thrill or hosting an extreme event; it's about embracing a mindset that cherishes the unconventional. This bride views her wedding not as a mere event but as a grand adventure, a journey into a lifetime of love marked by moments that echo the untamed beauty of nature.

For the adventurous bride, the allure of the outdoors is more than a picturesque setting; it's a canvas upon which her love story unfolds. She envisions saying "I do" surrounded by the breathtaking backdrop of a mountain range, on a secluded beach with waves serenading their commitment, or under the shade of ancient trees witnessing a love that stands the test of time.

But it's not just the location that defines her; it's the desire for a wedding that mirrors her values. The adventurous bride values experiences over extravagance, personal connections over grandeur. She seeks a celebration that feels authentic, a reflection of who she is as an individual and who they are as a couple.

For her, an adventurous wedding isn't about conforming to societal expectations but about breaking free from them. It's about dancing to the beat of her own heart, choosing a path that aligns with her spirit rather than adhering to tradition for tradition's sake. This bride embraces the idea that her wedding can be an extension of her personality, a celebration that embodies the joy of living life on her terms.

The adventurous bride is a visionary, seeing beyond the conventional notions of weddings. She is unafraid to challenge norms, welcoming the idea of a ceremony that mirrors the wild beauty of her love. Her adventurous spirit extends beyond the wedding day; it's a lifelong commitment to infuse every day with the same passion, spontaneity, and love for exploration that she brings to her wedding.

In the chapters ahead, we'll delve deeper into the mind of the adventurous bride, exploring the intricacies of planning an elopement that mirrors her spirit. From choosing the perfect outdoor location to navigating the legalities and permits, we'll be your guide on this journey into the heart of adventurous love. So, if you find yourself resonating with the thrill of the extraordinary, if you're ready to embrace the outdoors as your wedding canvas, then consider this guide your compass on the adventure of a lifetime.

Exploring the mindset of a bride who seeks an outdoor elopement

Let's take a stroll through the intricate landscape of the adventurous bride's mind—a terrain marked by a distinct mindset that finds solace, excitement, and purpose in the embrace of the great outdoors. It's not merely about choosing a scenic backdrop; it's about aligning the ceremony with a philosophy that values experiences over extravagance, intimacy over spectacle.

First and foremost, the adventurous bride is fueled by a profound love for nature. She finds inspiration in the rustle of leaves, the dance of wildflowers, and the melody of flowing rivers. For her, the outdoors are not just a setting; they're a source of energy, a sanctuary where she feels most connected to herself and her partner. The idea of intertwining this love for nature with the celebration of her commitment is not just appealing; it's an essential part of her vision.

This bride craves authenticity. The traditional ballroom setting, while beautiful for some, doesn't resonate with her spirit. She seeks a celebration that mirrors her identity, a reflection of her values and the unique connection she shares with her partner. The outdoors offer a blank canvas, allowing her to paint a wedding portrait that's uniquely hers. From the rustically charming to the majestically wild, the possibilities in nature are as diverse as her love story.

In the adventurous bride's mindset, there's a desire for something more profound than the conventional wedding spectacle. It's about crafting an experience that transcends the ordinary, one where the natural elements become witnesses and participants in the sacred exchange of vows. For her, the wind carries the whispers of promises, the trees stand witness to declarations of love, and the landscape becomes a silent storyteller of their journey together.

This mindset is not one that fears the unknown; rather, it embraces it with open arms. The unpredictable weather, the potential challenges of an outdoor setting—these are not deterrents but rather opportunities for spontaneity and adventure. The adventurous bride understands that life, much like nature, is beautifully unpredictable, and weaving that unpredictability into her wedding day is a celebration of the genuine, the unscripted, and the raw beauty of love.

Furthermore, this mindset cherishes the idea of a more intimate celebration. It's not about hosting a grand spectacle for the world to see; it's about sharing a profound moment with a select group of loved ones or even just the two souls deeply intertwined. The outdoors offer a stage where the focus remains on the essence of the commitment, undistracted by the grandeur of a traditional ceremony.

As we navigate deeper into the chapters ahead, we'll continue to unravel the layers of this mindset, exploring how it shapes every decision in the planning process. From choosing the right location to infusing personal touches into the ceremony, we'll be your guide in understanding and embracing the adventurous bride's unique perspective—one that turns a wedding into a grand adventure, a love story told against the backdrop of nature's awe-inspiring beauty.

Embracing the beauty of nature in wedding celebrations

In the heart of an outdoor wedding celebration beats the rhythm of nature's beauty, and for the adventurous bride, this heartbeat is the very soul of her vision. It's not just about selecting a scenic location; it's about weaving the inherent beauty of nature into the fabric of the entire celebration. Let's delve into the art of embracing this beauty and allowing it to paint the canvas of the wedding day.

Nature, in all its forms, holds a special place in the adventurous bride's heart. It's the silent partner in her love story, an integral element that transforms the ceremony into a living, breathing experience. The beauty of a mountainside, the tranquility of a forest clearing, or the rhythmic waves of an ocean—these are not just backdrops; they are co-creators of the wedding narrative, adding depth and resonance to the vows exchanged.

For the adventurous bride, nature becomes an ally in creating a sensory-rich experience. The scent of pine in the air, the touch of grass beneath their feet, the symphony of birdsong—these elements become part of the ceremony's poetry, enhancing not just the visual aesthetics but also the overall ambiance. It's an immersive experience that transcends the traditional confines of a wedding venue, inviting the couple and their guests to be fully present in the moment.

Embracing the beauty of nature also means acknowledging its impermanence. Unlike the controlled environment of an indoor venue, nature brings with it an ever-changing landscape. The shifting sunlight, the breeze that carries the scent of blooming flowers, or even an unexpected shower—all these elements contribute to the spontaneity and uniqueness of the celebration. The adventurous bride doesn't fear these changes; she welcomes them as part of the dynamic dance with the natural world.

In this celebration, the beauty of nature isn't confined to the ceremony alone. It permeates every aspect of the day, from pre-wedding adventures to post-ceremony celebrations. Picture hiking trails leading to hidden ceremony spots, or beachside picnics as the sun dips below the horizon. These are not just activities; they are extensions of the celebration, opportunities to revel in the beauty that surrounds them and to create lasting memories immersed in the magic of nature.

Furthermore, nature becomes a storyteller in its own right. Every tree, every rock, every vista holds a story, and the adventurous bride understands the significance of incorporating these natural elements into the ceremony. From incorporating local flora into the decor to choosing a location with historical or sentimental value, every decision is an intentional nod to the rich tapestry of nature's narrative.

As we navigate through the chapters ahead, we'll continue to explore how to not only choose a location but to truly commune with the beauty of nature. We'll uncover ways to let nature guide the aesthetic choices, infusing the celebration with authenticity and creating a wedding day that not only captures the eye but also speaks to the soul—a celebration that, like nature itself, is timeless, ever-changing, and eternally beautiful.

The Appeal of Outdoor Elopements

Imagine this: a vast sky above, the earth beneath your feet, and the soothing symphony of nature as the soundtrack to your commitment. That's the allure, the magnetic pull that draws the adventurous bride toward outdoor elopements. In this section, let's unravel the enchanting appeal that these natural settings hold and why they resonate so deeply with those who seek a celebration beyond the conventional.

First and foremost, it's about the canvas. The great outdoors offer a canvas that is boundless, ever-changing, and breathtakingly beautiful. From mountain peaks to tranquil beaches, from ancient forests to open meadows, the options are as diverse as love itself. This vast array of landscapes allows couples to curate a backdrop that not only mirrors their personalities but also becomes an integral part of the love story they're narrating.

The appeal extends beyond the aesthetic to a deeper, more personal connection. Nature has a unique way of grounding us, of connecting us to something larger than ourselves. For the adventurous bride, an outdoor elopement is not just a ceremony; it's a communion with the elements, a chance to exchange vows in a space that feels inherently sacred. The grandeur of nature becomes a metaphor for the grandeur of their commitment.

Moreover, there's an inherent intimacy in outdoor settings. Unlike large, traditional venues, the great outdoors invite couples to be close, physically and emotionally. Whether it's standing on a windswept cliff or sitting together on a sunlit meadow, the closeness to nature amplifies the closeness between the couple. It's an invitation to share not just vows but whispers, not just glances but silent moments of connection.

Then there's the element of adventure. Outdoor elopements are, by nature, more adventurous. They require a willingness to embrace the unpredictability of weather, to navigate through natural terrain, and to let go of the scripted nature of traditional weddings. This sense of adventure adds a layer of excitement to the celebration, making it not just a ceremony but an experience that the couple and their guests actively participate in.

The appeal also lies in the simplicity of it all. Outdoor elopements strip away the excess, the elaborate setups, and the unnecessary frills. What remains is a celebration in its purest form—two individuals, their love, and the beauty that surrounds them. It's a return to the essence of weddings, a focus on the couple and the commitment they are making.

Lastly, there's a timeless quality to outdoor elopements. Unlike trends that come and go, the beauty of nature is enduring. Choosing an outdoor setting creates a backdrop that transcends the constraints of time, allowing the couple to look back on their photos and relive the timeless magic of that day. It's a celebration that doesn't succumb to the ebb and flow of trends but remains eternally relevant and resonant.

As we venture into the upcoming chapters, we'll continue to explore and celebrate the myriad reasons why outdoor elopements hold such a magnetic allure. From the visual poetry of nature to the profound connection it fosters, we'll unravel the layers of this appeal, guiding you on a journey to create a wedding celebration that not only reflects your love but also embraces the enchanting beauty of the great outdoors.

Connecting with nature as a couple

In the heart of an outdoor elopement beats the rhythm of a couple intimately connected to nature, a couple whose love story intertwines seamlessly with the elements. This connection with nature isn't just a backdrop; it's an integral part of the narrative, a silent witness to the unique bond they share.

Picture this: a couple standing on the edge of a cliff, hand in hand, gazing out at the vast expanse before them. The wind carries with it the scent of adventure, and as they exchange vows, the rustle of leaves and the whispering breeze become the harmonious chorus to their commitment. It's a moment of profound connection, not just between the couple but between their love and the natural world.

Connecting with nature as a couple isn't just about choosing a pretty location; it's about immersing oneself in the environment, becoming an active participant in the grand tapestry of the outdoors. Whether it's hiking through dense forests, strolling along a secluded beach, or simply sitting beneath the shade of ancient trees, these shared experiences become the threads that weave their story.

For the adventurous couple, nature becomes a playground for their love, a canvas upon which they can express their deepest emotions. The rugged terrain, the gentle caress of a mountain breeze, or the warmth of sun-kissed meadows—these elements aren't just scenery; they're partners in the dance of their relationship. Each outdoor setting becomes a chapter in their love story, a snapshot of a moment shared against the backdrop of the natural world.

There's a sense of vulnerability and authenticity that comes with connecting in nature. Unlike the controlled environment of a traditional venue, the outdoors present an unfiltered, unscripted space. The couple isn't shielded by walls; they are embraced by the vastness of the landscape. This vulnerability fosters a deeper connection, as they navigate the unpredictability of weather, overcome challenges, and revel in the spontaneity of the moment.

Moreover, nature becomes a metaphor for the couple's journey. Just as the landscape changes and evolves, so does their relationship. The ebb and flow of the natural world mirror the seasons of their love, and every outdoor adventure becomes a symbolic step in their shared odyssey. It's an acknowledgment that, like nature, love is a dynamic force, ever-changing, ever-growing.

In the midst of nature, couples find a sanctuary for meaningful conversations. Whether it's a quiet conversation by a bubbling stream or a laughter-filled exchange on a sunlit hill, these moments of connection become the building blocks of their intimacy. Nature provides the backdrop, but it's the couple who infuses the scene with the emotions, the laughter, and the unspoken understanding that defines their bond.

As we navigate through the chapters ahead, we'll delve deeper into the ways in which couples can not only choose a location but truly connect with the natural setting. From pre-wedding adventures to post-ceremony reflections, we'll explore how nature becomes not just a venue but a companion in the couple's journey, an active participant in the celebration of their love. So, if you're yearning for a wedding that goes beyond the ordinary, one where your love story becomes entwined with the beauty of nature, then consider this guide your compass on the path to a truly extraordinary celebration.

Navigating the Contents of this Guide

Congratulations on embarking on this exciting journey into the heart of outdoor elopements! As we set the stage for the adventure that lies ahead, let's take a moment to navigate the contents of this guide and discover the treasures it holds for the adventurous bride.

Consider this guide your compass, guiding you through the intricate and awe-inspiring landscape of planning an outdoor elopement. It's not just about choosing a location; it's about crafting an experience that resonates with the spirit of adventure and the love you share. So, what can you expect to find within these pages?

We begin by defining the adventurous bride, exploring the mindset that fuels her desire for an outdoor celebration. We delve into what makes her unique, why she's drawn to nature, and how this mindset shapes the entire elopement experience. It's about understanding the essence of the adventurous spirit and how it intertwines with the beauty of the great outdoors.

Moving forward, we explore the appeal of outdoor elopements. What is it about these natural settings that captivates the adventurous bride's heart? From the limitless canvas of landscapes to the sense of intimacy and adventure, we unravel the layers of this allure. It's a celebration that goes beyond the conventional, offering a timeless, genuine, and enchanting experience.

One key aspect we delve into is the connection with nature as a couple. Nature becomes more than a setting; it becomes an active participant in the love story. Whether it's sharing adventures, embracing vulnerability, or finding metaphors in the landscape, we uncover the ways in which couples can truly connect with the natural world and make it an integral part of their celebration.

Now, as we stand on the precipice of this adventure, it's crucial to address the practical aspects. Chapter 2 tackled choosing the perfect outdoor location, considering personal preferences, legalities, permits, accessibility, and logistics. It's about finding a place that not only speaks to your heart but also aligns with the practicalities of hosting a ceremony in the great outdoors.

Chapter 3 delves into weather considerations, acknowledging the unpredictable yet enchanting element of nature. From understanding seasons and climates to crafting backup plans that enhance rather than hinder the celebration, we equip you with the tools to navigate the ever-changing weather and create a day filled with magic.

Looking ahead, we explore the art of crafting an adventure-packed itinerary in Chapter 4. From pre-wedding adventures to the ceremony and post-ceremony celebrations, we guide you in striking the perfect balance between adventure and intimacy. It's about turning the entire day into a journey, a celebration of love infused with the thrill of exploration.

As we continue this journey together, anticipate discovering more about photography and memories in Chapter 5. From choosing the right photographer to capturing candid moments and preserving outdoor memories, we unravel the secrets to creating a visual narrative that mirrors the essence of your outdoor elopement.

Subsequent chapters dive into attire and style, personalizing your outdoor ceremony, navigating family and friends, embracing a budget-friendly approach, and reflecting on the post-elopement experience. Each chapter is a step on this adventurous path, offering insights, tips, and inspiration tailored for the bride who seeks a celebration that mirrors her spirit.

So, as you embark on this guide, let your curiosity lead the way. Dive into the chapters that resonate with you, glean inspiration from the real-life elopement stories, and use the provided resources to craft a celebration that not only embraces the beauty of nature but also becomes a reflection of your unique love story. Cheers to the journey ahead!

Setting expectations for your elopement journey

As you embark on the exciting journey of planning your outdoor elopement, let's take a moment to set expectations and lay the foundation for the adventure ahead. Think of this as a friendly chat, a heart-to-heart conversation that helps you navigate the twists and turns of this elopement journey with confidence and joy.

First and foremost, embrace the spirit of flexibility. Planning an outdoor elopement is a dance with nature, and like any good dance, it requires adaptability. Weather can be unpredictable, and landscapes, though breathtaking, may present unexpected challenges. Setting the expectation for flexibility allows you to flow with the rhythm of the day, turning unforeseen circumstances into opportunities for spontaneity and magic.

Another key aspect to consider is the collaborative nature of this journey. While this guide is your trusty companion, remember that you are not alone in the planning process. Engage with your partner, communicate openly, and involve each other in decisions. Your love story is a joint venture, and planning your elopement should be a shared experience that strengthens the bond between you.

Moreover, as you navigate through the chapters, understand that the goal is not perfection but authenticity. Embrace the imperfections, and view them as unique brushstrokes on the canvas of your love story. Nature, after all, is beautifully imperfect, and your elopement can reflect the same genuine beauty.

Let's also talk about the balance between adventure and intimacy. Your outdoor elopement is an adventure, a celebration of love in the midst of nature's grandeur. However, it's equally important to infuse moments of intimacy and connection. Finding this balance will make your elopement not just a grand event but a deeply personal and meaningful experience.

Consider this journey a celebration of love that extends beyond the wedding day. The chapters unfold not just as a guide for planning the ceremony but as an invitation to explore and deepen your connection with each other. The memories you create during the planning process become part of your love story, adding richness to the narrative you'll share for a lifetime.

As you read through the chapters, remember that there's no one-size-fits-all approach. Your love story is unique, and your elopement should reflect that. Feel free to adapt the advice, glean inspiration, and tailor it to suit your preferences. This journey is about discovering what resonates with you and weaving those elements into the tapestry of your celebration.

Lastly, savor the process. The journey itself is a celebration, filled with moments of joy, discovery, and shared excitement. From choosing a location that speaks to your hearts to crafting personalized details that reflect your personalities, relish each step. The joy lies not only in reaching the destination but also in the path that leads you there.

So, as you turn the pages of this guide, do so with a heart open to adventure, a spirit ready to embrace the unexpected, and a commitment to weaving your love story into the very fabric of nature. This journey is yours, and the guide is here to illuminate the path, offering insights, inspiration, and companionship as you create a celebration that mirrors the extraordinary love you share. Cheers to the adventure that awaits you!

Chapter 2: Choosing the Perfect Outdoor Location

Welcome to Chapter 2, where the journey to your dream outdoor elopement truly begins! Choosing the perfect location is like selecting the setting for a magnificent story—it sets the tone, evokes emotions, and becomes the canvas upon which your love story unfolds. In this chapter, we'll embark on a delightful exploration, guiding you through the enchanting process of finding the outdoor location that resonates with your hearts.

Think of your chosen location as more than just a backdrop; it's a co-author in the narrative of your love. Whether you envision saying your vows with the mountain breeze in your hair, beneath the towering trees of a lush forest, or by the rhythmic waves of the ocean, the possibilities are as boundless as your love.

We'll delve into the intricacies of aligning your personal preferences with the practical considerations of hosting an outdoor ceremony. From the legalities and permits to accessibility and logistics, we'll navigate the landscape of choosing a location that not only steals your breath away but also ensures a smooth and stress-free celebration.

As we embark on this journey together, keep in mind that your chosen location is a reflection of your unique love story. It's a place that speaks to your souls, where nature becomes an active participant in the sacred exchange of vows. So, let's dive into the adventure of discovering the perfect outdoor setting—one that resonates with your spirit, encapsulates the essence of your love, and sets the stage for a celebration that's as extraordinary as your journey together. Get ready to be inspired, enchanted, and guided toward the outdoor location of your dreams. The next chapter of your love story awaits!

Reflecting on Personal Preferences

As you stand at the threshold of choosing the perfect outdoor location for your elopement, let's start by delving into the rich tapestry of your personal preferences. Your love story is unique, and the setting you choose should be a mirror reflecting the essence of your relationship.

Consider the elements that resonate with you as a couple. Reflect on your shared experiences, favorite moments, and the places that hold special significance in your journey together. Perhaps it's a mountaintop where you shared your first sunrise, a beach where the waves witnessed your laughter, or a forest where you found solace in each other's company. These personal touchpoints become the foundation for selecting a location that not only appeals visually but also resonates emotionally.

Think about the atmosphere you envision for your ceremony. Are you drawn to the serenity of a quiet meadow, the grandeur of a majestic cliff, or the rhythmic sounds of a lakeside shore? The ambiance of your chosen location should align with the mood you desire for your celebration. Whether it's an intimate and secluded setting or a more open and expansive space, your preferences will guide you toward a location that feels like an extension of your love story.

Consider your hobbies and interests as a couple. Are you avid hikers, adventure seekers, or beach lovers? Let these shared passions influence your choice of location. If you both find solace in the great outdoors, selecting a location that reflects your shared interests will make your elopement not just a ceremony but an authentic representation of who you are as a couple.

Moreover, think about the style and theme you want for your celebration. Do you envision a bohemian, rustic, or minimalist aesthetic? Your personal style should seamlessly integrate with the chosen location, creating a harmonious visual narrative. Whether it's the raw beauty of a desert landscape, the lush greenery of a forest, or the simplicity of a beach, your preferences will guide you toward a location that complements your desired theme.

Reflecting on personal preferences isn't just about selecting a visually stunning location; it's about choosing a place that feels like an extension of your love. It's about finding a setting that speaks to your hearts, captures the nuances of your relationship, and becomes a character in the love story you're telling.

As you navigate through the process of reflecting on your personal preferences, keep in mind that there are no right or wrong choices—only those that resonate authentically with you. The journey of choosing the perfect outdoor location is an exploration of your love story, a delightful adventure that unfolds as you align your personal preferences with the vast and breathtaking possibilities that nature offers. So, take a moment to reflect, envision, and let your hearts guide you toward the outdoor location that will become the stage for your extraordinary love story.

Identifying individual preferences in natural settings

As we dive deeper into the process of choosing the perfect outdoor location for your elopement, let's narrow our focus to identifying individual preferences within natural settings. Nature, with its diverse landscapes, offers a plethora of options, each with its own unique charm. This section aims to help you pinpoint the specific elements that resonate with you and your partner, guiding you toward a location that aligns seamlessly with your individual preferences.

Consider the type of natural setting that speaks to your heart. Are you captivated by the grandeur of mountains, the tranquility of forests, the vastness of deserts, or the rhythmic embrace of the ocean? Your individual preferences will shape the backdrop of your elopement, creating a setting that feels not only visually stunning but emotionally resonant.

Think about the elements of nature that evoke a sense of connection and joy. Is it the rustling leaves of a wooded glen, the fragrance of wildflowers in a meadow, or the sound of waves crashing on a rocky shore? Identifying these specific natural elements allows you to personalize your choice, creating a location that engages not only your sight but all your senses.

Consider the time of day that holds a special allure for you. Does the idea of exchanging vows beneath the golden hues of a sunrise, basking in the warmth of midday sunlight, or experiencing the enchantment of a sunset ceremony capture your imagination? Your preferred time of day will influence not only the aesthetics but also the overall atmosphere of your chosen location.

Reflect on the scale and intimacy you desire. Do you envision an expansive, open space where the sky seems to stretch endlessly, or do you prefer a more intimate setting nestled within the embrace of nature's nooks and crannies? Your preference for scale will guide you toward locations that offer the space and intimacy you envision for your elopement.

Consider the level of adventure you seek. Are you drawn to locations that require a hike, a climb, or a boat ride to reach, or do you prefer a spot easily accessible by a short walk? Your individual appetite for adventure will shape not only the location but also the overall experience of your elopement.

Think about the season that resonates with you. Does the idea of a snowy winter wonderland, a blossoming spring landscape, a sun-kissed summer ceremony, or the vibrant colors of autumn capture your heart? Your preferred season will not only influence the visual aesthetics but also the overall mood and atmosphere of your celebration.

Moreover, consider any cultural or sentimental preferences that hold significance for you and your partner. Is there a specific type of nature that holds cultural importance, or perhaps a location with sentimental value that you both share? Identifying these individual preferences will infuse your chosen location with layers of meaning and connection.

As you navigate through the process of identifying individual preferences within natural settings, remember that the goal is to create a location that feels like an authentic extension of your love story. It's about finding a place that not only visually captivates but also emotionally resonates, creating a setting that becomes an integral part of the beautiful narrative you're weaving together. So, reflect on these elements, discuss them with your partner, and let your collective preferences guide you toward the outdoor location that mirrors the unique beauty of your love.

Legalities and Permits

As you embark on the thrilling journey of choosing the perfect outdoor location for your elopement, it's essential to delve into the practical aspects of legalities and permits. While nature's beauty may seem boundless, navigating the legal landscape ensures a smooth and stress-free celebration. Consider this a friendly guide through the paperwork and permissions, allowing you to focus on the joyous moments of your ceremony.

Start by understanding the legal requirements associated with outdoor ceremonies in your chosen location. Different areas may have specific regulations governing events held in natural settings. It's crucial to research and familiarize yourself with the local laws, ensuring that your elopement complies with any necessary permits, licenses, or restrictions.

Reach out to local authorities or park services to inquire about the specific requirements for hosting an event in your desired outdoor location. They can provide valuable information on necessary permits, any associated fees, and guidelines to follow. Engaging in open communication with these entities not only ensures compliance but also fosters a positive relationship, making the process smoother.

Consider the logistics of obtaining permits for your chosen location. Some areas may have a straightforward application process, while others might involve more detailed documentation. Be sure to start this process well in advance to allow for any processing times and to secure your desired date. Early preparation is key to avoiding last-minute hurdles and ensuring a seamless experience.

Understand any restrictions or limitations that may apply to your chosen location. Some areas might have specific rules regarding the number of attendees, noise levels, or even the use of certain equipment. Being aware of these restrictions allows you to plan accordingly and create a celebration that aligns with the guidelines set forth.

In addition to local regulations, consider any federal or state requirements that may impact your elopement. Certain natural settings fall under the jurisdiction of national parks or protected areas, each with its own set of rules and regulations. Researching and adhering to these broader guidelines is essential for a smooth and lawful celebration.

While legalities may seem like a daunting aspect of the planning process, they serve as safeguards to ensure the safety and enjoyment of both you and your guests. By approaching this aspect with a proactive and organized mindset, you can transform it into a manageable and stress-free part of your elopement journey.

Engage with local vendors or experienced professionals who are familiar with the legal landscape of your chosen location. Wedding planners, photographers, or even local officiants often possess valuable insights and can provide guidance based on their experiences. Their expertise can be an invaluable resource as you navigate the intricacies of permits and legal requirements.

In conclusion, while legalities and permits may not be the most glamorous aspects of planning your elopement, they are crucial for creating a celebration that is not only beautiful but also compliant with local regulations. By approaching this process with diligence, early preparation, and a willingness to engage with the necessary authorities, you'll pave the way for a seamless and joyous outdoor ceremony, surrounded by the breathtaking beauty of nature.

Researching and obtaining necessary permits

Embarking on the journey to bring your outdoor elopement dreams to life involves more than just selecting a picturesque location. Once you've set your sights on the perfect natural setting, it's time to delve into the practical world of permits. While this might sound bureaucratic, think of it as the backstage pass that ensures your celebration unfolds smoothly within the bounds of legality and consideration for the environment.

Start by conducting thorough research into the specific permits required for your chosen location. Different areas have varying regulations, and understanding the unique requirements of your selected natural setting is key. Reach out to local authorities, park services, or relevant governing bodies to gather comprehensive information on the necessary permits, associated fees, and any additional conditions.

In your pursuit of permits, consider engaging in open communication with the entities responsible for issuing them. This isn't merely a bureaucratic formality; it's an opportunity to establish a positive and collaborative relationship. Seek to understand not just the legal requirements but also the nuances and considerations that will contribute to the success of your elopement.

Early preparation is paramount. Commence the permit application process well in advance to allow for any potential delays. Popular outdoor locations often have high demand for events, and securing your desired date requires a proactive approach. Treat the permit application as a priority to avoid last-minute stress and ensure a seamless path toward obtaining the necessary approvals.

When delving into the permit application, be diligent and detail-oriented. Provide all required documentation accurately and promptly. This not only expedites the process but also demonstrates your commitment to adhering to regulations. Thoroughness in your application reflects your dedication to creating an event that respects both the natural environment and local guidelines.

Consider seeking assistance from professionals experienced in navigating permit processes. Local wedding planners, photographers, or officiants often possess insights into the specific requirements of your chosen location. Their expertise can guide you through the intricacies of the permit application, offering valuable advice and helping you avoid potential pitfalls.

Keep in mind that the permit application is not merely a formality but a commitment to responsible event planning. It ensures that your elopement aligns with environmental and legal considerations, contributing to the sustainability of outdoor celebrations. Embrace the process as an opportunity to be conscientious stewards of the natural beauty that will serve as the backdrop to your love story.

Remember that each location is unique, and permit requirements may vary widely. Whether it's a beach, mountain, forest, or any other natural setting, approach the permit process with an open mind and a willingness to adapt. Flexibility and collaboration with local authorities contribute to a positive experience for all involved.

As you navigate the path to obtaining necessary permits, view it as a partnership with the natural environment and local community. The permits serve as a means to ensure that your celebration leaves a positive impact, not only on your memories but also on the delicate ecosystems that surround your chosen outdoor haven. So, with enthusiasm, diligence, and a dash of patience, embark on this permit journey as an essential step toward crafting the outdoor elopement of your dreams.

Understanding legal requirements for outdoor ceremonies

Understanding the legal requirements for your outdoor ceremony is like deciphering the hidden language that ensures your celebration unfolds seamlessly within the bounds of the law. As you navigate this aspect of planning, consider it a thoughtful dance, where compliance and celebration twirl hand in hand.

Begin by immersing yourself in the specific legal requirements governing outdoor ceremonies in your chosen location. Local regulations can vary widely, and getting acquainted with the unique stipulations of your selected natural setting is essential. Reach out to local authorities, park services, or relevant governing bodies to gain a comprehensive understanding of the legal landscape.

Pay attention to any permits or licenses that may be required for hosting an event in your chosen outdoor location. These documents serve as the official stamp of approval, granting you permission to celebrate in the embrace of nature. Understanding the intricacies of the permit process ensures that your event complies with local laws and regulations.

Consider any restrictions or limitations that may be in place. Some areas might have specific rules regarding the number of attendees, noise levels, or even the use of certain equipment. Familiarize yourself with these details, as they will shape the logistics of your celebration and contribute to a harmonious experience for both you and the natural surroundings.

Furthermore, explore whether there are any specific guidelines for waste disposal, signage, or other considerations outlined by local authorities. Adopting environmentally conscious practices aligns your celebration with the principles of sustainability and ensures that your event leaves minimal impact on the natural beauty of the location.

Engage in open communication with the entities responsible for enforcing these legal requirements. Treat this as an opportunity to not only gather information but also to build a positive relationship. Authorities are often willing to provide guidance and support to ensure that your outdoor ceremony adheres to the necessary legal standards.

As you sift through the legalities, consider seeking assistance from professionals familiar with the landscape. Wedding planners, photographers, or officiants experienced in the region can offer valuable insights into the legal nuances of your chosen location. Their expertise becomes an invaluable resource, guiding you through the complexities and ensuring a smooth journey toward compliance.

Remember that legal requirements aren't meant to hinder your celebration but to safeguard both you and the natural environment. Embrace these guidelines as a means to create a joyful and responsible event. As you work within the legal framework, you contribute to the sustainability of outdoor celebrations, leaving a positive legacy for future couples seeking to immerse themselves in nature's beauty.

Approach the understanding of legal requirements not as a hurdle but as a crucial part of the dance that makes your outdoor celebration possible. By appreciating the intricacies of compliance, you not only ensure the legality of your event but also pave the way for an unforgettable and conscientious experience. So, with a blend of enthusiasm and understanding, waltz through the legal landscape, confident that your outdoor ceremony will harmonize beautifully with the laws that govern it.

Accessibility and Logistics

Navigating the realms of accessibility and logistics is akin to charting the course for your outdoor elopement adventure. While the allure of nature beckons, understanding the practicalities ensures that your chosen location is not just breathtaking but also accessible and accommodating for you, your guests, and the professionals involved in making your celebration a reality.

Start by considering the accessibility of your chosen outdoor location. How easily can you and your guests reach the site? Assess the terrain, pathways, and any potential obstacles that might impact the journey. Whether it's a mountaintop, beach, or forest, understanding the accessibility sets the foundation for a smooth and enjoyable experience.

Think about the comfort and convenience of your guests. If your chosen location involves a hike or requires special transportation, consider how this might impact your attendees. Providing clear information about the level of accessibility ensures that your loved ones can fully participate in and enjoy the celebration. This thoughtful approach contributes to the overall positive experience for everyone involved.

Explore the logistics of setting up and managing your outdoor ceremony. Are there designated areas for ceremonies, or do you have the flexibility to choose your preferred spot? Understanding the logistics allows you to plan the layout, seating arrangements, and any additional elements that will enhance the ambiance of your chosen location.

Consider the availability of amenities. Depending on the remoteness of your chosen spot, amenities such as restrooms, water sources, or shelter may vary. Being aware of these factors helps you plan and communicate effectively with your guests. Consider providing necessary information, such as whether restroom facilities will be available or if guests should bring water bottles.

Engage with local professionals who are familiar with the logistics of your chosen location. Local vendors, photographers, or wedding planners often possess insights into the practical aspects that can impact your celebration. Their expertise can guide you in making informed decisions and navigating any challenges that may arise.

Think about the timing of your ceremony, especially if your chosen location has specific opening or closing hours. Consider the sunset or sunrise times, as they can significantly influence the lighting and overall atmosphere of your celebration. Understanding these temporal aspects allows you to plan a ceremony that aligns seamlessly with the natural rhythm of the location.

Anticipate the potential impact of weather on accessibility and logistics. While you can't control the elements, having contingency plans in place ensures that your celebration remains resilient in the face of unforeseen changes. Whether it's rain, wind, or unexpected temperature fluctuations, preparing for weather-related scenarios enhances your ability to adapt and ensures a memorable experience.

Incorporate a sense of adventure into your planning. While accessibility and logistics are crucial considerations, they are also part of the excitement of an outdoor elopement. Embrace the journey, celebrate the uniqueness of your chosen location, and view each logistical aspect as an opportunity to add character and charm to your celebration.

In conclusion, the dance between accessibility and logistics is a harmonious one, ensuring that your outdoor elopement unfolds seamlessly and joyously. By understanding the practicalities of your chosen location, you create an experience that not only captivates with natural beauty but also delights with thoughtful planning. So, as you venture into the logistics of your outdoor celebration, let the spirit of adventure guide you, and relish in the anticipation of a ceremony that blends seamlessly with the charm of the great outdoors.

Evaluating accessibility for the couple and guests

As you embark on the journey to choose the perfect outdoor location for your elopement, it's essential to evaluate accessibility not just for yourselves but for your cherished guests as well. This consideration ensures that everyone can fully participate in the celebration, sharing in the joy of your love amid the stunning backdrop of nature.

Start by assessing the ease of access for you and your partner. Consider the level of physical activity and any potential challenges you may encounter. Whether you're envisioning an intimate mountaintop ceremony, a beachfront exchange of vows, or a forest enclave for your celebration, understanding the physical demands sets the stage for a memorable experience.

Extend your evaluation to include the accessibility for your guests. Imagine the journey they will undertake to witness and partake in your love story. If your chosen location involves a hike, consider the trail's difficulty and duration. Providing clear information about the level of physical activity required allows your guests to make informed decisions about their participation.

Communicate openly with your guests about any potential challenges they may encounter. If your chosen location is remote or involves special transportation, such as a boat ride or off-road access, make sure to provide detailed information in advance. This transparency ensures that your loved ones can plan accordingly, enhancing their overall experience.

Explore options to enhance accessibility for your guests. Depending on the location, you may have the opportunity to arrange alternative transportation or provide assistance for those with mobility considerations. Collaborate with local professionals who can offer insights and solutions to make your chosen spot as accessible and accommodating as possible.

Consider the availability of amenities at your chosen location. Restrooms, water sources, and shaded areas can significantly impact the comfort of your guests. If these amenities are limited, communicate this information clearly and consider providing alternatives, such as portable restrooms or hydration stations, to ensure everyone's well-being during the celebration.

Engage with local professionals who understand the intricacies of accessibility in your chosen region. Local vendors, photographers, or wedding planners can offer valuable insights into the practical considerations that may impact the journey for both you and your guests. Their familiarity with the local landscape enhances your ability to plan and execute a celebration that is both stunning and accessible.

Timing plays a crucial role in accessibility, particularly if your chosen location has specific opening or closing hours. Consider the timing of your ceremony in relation to the accessibility of the site. If your celebration coincides with sunrise or sunset, ensure that your guests have ample time to navigate the location safely, especially if the trail or access points are affected by low light conditions.

While evaluating accessibility, embrace the spirit of adventure that comes with an outdoor elopement. Communicate your excitement for the unique aspects of your chosen location, and invite your guests to share in the joy of exploration. By fostering an inclusive and transparent approach to accessibility, you create a celebration that not only captivates with natural beauty but also resonates with the warmth of shared experiences. So, as you embark on this evaluation, envision a celebration that welcomes everyone into the heart of your love story, surrounded by the breathtaking allure of nature.

Planning logistics for a smooth outdoor celebration

Planning logistics for your outdoor celebration is akin to orchestrating a symphony where every note, from the initial preparations to the final crescendo, contributes to the harmonious melody of your special day. As you navigate the practicalities, envision a seamless experience that not only captures the essence of your love but also ensures the comfort and enjoyment of all involved.

Consider the layout of your outdoor ceremony space. Whether it's a beach, mountain clearing, or forest glade, visualize the flow of the celebration. Imagine where you and your partner will stand, where guests will be seated, and any additional elements you wish to incorporate, such as an altar or ceremonial decor. This mental map serves as the canvas upon which your love story will unfold.

Explore the logistics of setting up and dismantling your ceremony space. If your chosen location is a public space or nature reserve, inquire about any guidelines for temporary installations. Understanding the rules and responsibilities regarding setup ensures that your celebration is not only beautiful but also respectful of the environment.

Anticipate the timing of your ceremony in relation to accessibility and lighting conditions. If your location has specific opening or closing hours, plan your celebration accordingly. Similarly, if you've chosen a site renowned for its sunrise or sunset views, coordinate your ceremony to coincide with these magical moments, creating an atmosphere that is both visually stunning and romantically resonant.

Consider the availability of amenities for both you and your guests. If your chosen location is remote, think about practicalities such as restroom facilities, water sources, and shelter. If these amenities are limited, communicate this information to your guests in advance and consider providing alternatives to ensure everyone's comfort throughout the celebration.

Engage with local professionals who can offer insights into the logistics of your chosen location. Photographers, wedding planners, or vendors familiar with the region can provide valuable advice on navigating practical considerations. Their experience can guide you in making informed decisions, ensuring that your celebration unfolds smoothly.

Weather is an ever-present factor in outdoor ceremonies, and planning for it is an essential logistical consideration. Consider the season, historical weather patterns, and any potential changes that might occur. Having contingency plans for unexpected weather ensures that your celebration remains resilient and enjoyable, rain or shine.

Incorporate a timeline into your logistical planning. Consider the duration of your ceremony, any post-ceremony activities, and the overall flow of the celebration. Creating a loose timeline provides structure while allowing for the spontaneity and natural rhythm that come with outdoor events.

Extend your logistical planning to include transportation for you, your partner, and your guests. If your chosen location requires special transportation, such as a boat ride or off-road access, make arrangements in advance. Providing clear information about transportation options ensures that everyone arrives at the celebration with ease.

As you delve into the logistics of your outdoor celebration, envision a day where every detail aligns seamlessly, allowing you to fully immerse yourself in the joy of the moment. While logistics may seem like practicalities, they serve as the invisible threads that weave together the fabric of your love story. So, as you plan with enthusiasm and meticulous attention, picture a celebration that not only dazzles with natural beauty but also unfolds effortlessly, creating memories that will resonate for a lifetime.

Chapter 3: Weather Considerations

Welcome to Chapter 3, where we dive into the ever-changing and sometimes unpredictable world of weather considerations for your outdoor elopement. Just as your love story has its unique twists and turns, so does the atmospheric dance that surrounds your chosen celebration location. Weather, with its whimsical nature, adds an extra layer of enchantment to your special day, and understanding its nuances becomes an integral part of planning a memorable outdoor ceremony.

Picture this chapter as your trusty weather companion, here to guide you through the intricacies of the elements. Whether you're dreaming of exchanging vows under the warmth of the sun, the gentle mist of rain, or the soft glow of a cloudy sky, we'll explore how to embrace and prepare for the diverse weather conditions that may grace your celebration.

We'll unravel the secrets of seasonal variations, helping you navigate the unique qualities each season brings to your chosen location. From the blooming colors of spring to the warmth of summer, the vibrant hues of autumn, and the serene beauty of winter, each season presents its own palette, setting the stage for a celebration that harmonizes with the natural world.

As we embark on this weather-centric journey, consider this chapter your weather whisperer, providing insights, tips, and contingency plans to ensure that, come rain or shine, your outdoor elopement is a testament to the beauty of embracing nature's elements. Together, let's navigate the atmospheric symphony, creating a celebration that not only reflects the meteorological charm of your chosen location but also elevates your love story to new heights. So, buckle up for a meteorological adventure as we explore the intriguing and often whimsical world of weather considerations for your extraordinary outdoor elopement.

Seasons and Climate

As you plan your outdoor elopement, the seasons and climate of your chosen location become pivotal characters in the narrative of your celebration. Each season paints the landscape with its unique brush strokes, and understanding the nuances of these changes ensures that your love story harmonizes beautifully with the natural rhythm of the environment.

Let's start our journey by delving into the dance of the seasons. Spring, with its tender blossoms and vibrant greenery, symbolizes renewal and the beginning of new chapters. Choosing this season infuses your celebration with a sense of freshness and blooming romance. Imagine saying your vows amidst fields of wildflowers or under the canopy of cherry blossoms— a tapestry of colors unfolding as you embark on this beautiful journey together.

Summer, the season of warmth and long, sunlit days, invites you to bask in the golden glow of love. Picture exchanging vows on a sun-kissed beach or atop a hill with panoramic views. The balmy evenings offer the perfect backdrop for a celebration that lingers in the hearts of you and your guests, wrapped in the embrace of the summer sun.

Autumn, with its rich tapestry of reds, oranges, and golds, sets the stage for a celebration of warmth and coziness. The crisp air and falling leaves create an atmosphere of nostalgia and reflection. Imagine an elopement in a forest adorned with the hues of autumn, capturing the essence of your love as you embark on a journey reminiscent of a romantic fall day.

Winter, a season of quiet beauty and stark contrasts, transforms your celebration into a winter wonderland. Picture saying your vows against the backdrop of snow-covered landscapes or in a cozy cabin with a crackling fireplace. The serene beauty of winter creates a canvas for an intimate celebration, where the chill in the air is warmed by the glow of your love.

Understanding the climate of your chosen location further refines the palette of possibilities for your celebration. Coastal areas might offer a refreshing breeze, while mountainous regions may have cooler temperatures even in the summer. Deserts may boast warm days but cool nights, and forests could bring the chance of gentle rain. Your location's unique climate becomes a key player in determining the attire, timing, and overall atmosphere of your elopement.

As you navigate the seasons and climate, consider the unique qualities each brings to your celebration. Tailor your plans to embrace the inherent charm of your chosen time, whether it's the vibrant energy of spring, the sun-soaked days of summer, the nostalgic hues of autumn, or the serene beauty of winter. Embrace the ebb and flow of nature's cycles, letting the seasons and climate become integral elements that enrich the tapestry of your love story.

Remember, there's no right or wrong choice when it comes to the season of your elopement; it's about finding the time that resonates most with your love story. So, as you explore the seasons and climate of your chosen location, envision a celebration that aligns seamlessly with the natural beauty that each season brings, creating a timeless and atmospheric backdrop for the extraordinary love you're celebrating.

Exploring the pros and cons of each season

Embarking on the journey of choosing the season for your outdoor elopement is akin to selecting the perfect soundtrack for a movie – each season comes with its own set of pros and cons, and the key is finding the harmonious notes that resonate with your love story.

Let's begin our exploration with spring, a season synonymous with rebirth and blossoming beauty.

Picture vibrant wildflowers carpeting the landscape, trees adorned with delicate blooms, and a gentle breeze carrying the sweet scent of renewal. Spring brings a sense of freshness and the promise of new beginnings, creating an enchanting backdrop for your celebration. However, be mindful of potential rain showers that might sprinkle this season, and consider contingency plans to ensure your outdoor ceremony remains delightful, rain or shine.

Summer, with its sun-drenched days and balmy evenings, sets the stage for a celebration bathed in golden warmth. Imagine the sun casting a soft glow on your ceremony, the long daylight hours allowing for extended festivities, and the joyous atmosphere of a summer soirée. However, be mindful of the potential for higher temperatures, especially in certain regions. Consider providing shade, hydration stations, and lighter attire for you and your guests to ensure everyone stays comfortable and cool.

As we move to autumn, envision a celebration surrounded by the rich hues of red, orange, and gold. The crisp air and falling leaves create a cozy and romantic atmosphere. Autumn lends itself to rustic and warm décor, making it perfect for those seeking an elopement with a touch of nostalgia. However, be aware of the potential for cooler temperatures, and plan accordingly with warm attire and perhaps even blankets for your guests.

Winter, with its serene beauty and hushed landscapes, transforms your celebration into a magical winter wonderland. Picture saying your vows against the backdrop of snow-covered landscapes or in a cozy cabin with a crackling fireplace. The stillness and quiet beauty of winter create an intimate atmosphere, ideal for those desiring an elopement wrapped in a blanket of snow. However, be prepared for colder temperatures and potential challenges related to travel and accessibility in snowy conditions.

As you explore the pros and cons of each season, consider your personal preferences, the atmosphere you envision, and the unique qualities that resonate with your love story. Remember that flexibility and preparedness are key. Having contingency plans in place for unexpected weather variations ensures that your celebration remains resilient and enjoyable, regardless of the season's quirks.

Engage with local professionals who are familiar with the nuances of each season in your chosen location. Photographers, wedding planners, or vendors can offer valuable insights into how weather patterns may impact your celebration. Their expertise can guide you in making informed decisions, ensuring that the pros of your chosen season shine while mitigating any potential cons.

Ultimately, the season you choose becomes an integral part of your love story, shaping the atmosphere and ambiance of your outdoor elopement. So, as you weigh the pros and cons, envision a celebration that not only aligns with the natural beauty of the season but also becomes a timeless and atmospheric chapter in the extraordinary story of your love.

Adapting plans based on regional climates

As you plan your outdoor elopement, understanding and adapting to the regional climate of your chosen location is akin to tailoring a perfectly-fitted wedding gown. Each region boasts its unique atmospheric quirks, and by aligning your plans with the local climate, you ensure a celebration that not only feels natural but also allows you and your guests to revel in the beauty of the surroundings.

Coastal areas, with their proximity to the sea, bring a refreshing breeze and a maritime charm to your celebration. Picture exchanging vows with the sound of waves as your backdrop, the scent of salt in the air, and a gentle breeze carrying the whispers of the ocean. However, be prepared for potential windier conditions, and consider this in your choice of décor, hairstyles, and attire to ensure everything stays in place for a picture-perfect celebration.

Mountainous regions offer a majestic backdrop for your elopement, with sweeping vistas and crisp mountain air. Imagine saying your vows against a panoramic mountain view, the cool breeze adding a touch of invigorating freshness to your celebration. However, be mindful of potentially cooler temperatures, especially as the altitude increases. Provide warm attire for you and your guests, and consider blankets or wraps to keep everyone comfortable during the ceremony.

Desert locales, with their vast expanses and unique landscapes, create an otherworldly atmosphere for your celebration. Picture an elopement amidst golden dunes or red rock formations, bathed in the warm glow of the desert sun. However, be prepared for significant temperature variations between day and night. Plan accordingly with attire suitable for warmer daytime temperatures and cooler evenings, ensuring your celebration remains comfortable and enjoyable.

Forested areas, with their lush greenery and natural canopies, offer a serene and enchanting setting for your elopement. Imagine exchanging vows surrounded by towering trees, the dappled sunlight creating a magical ambiance. However, be aware of potential rain in forested regions, especially if your celebration is in a temperate climate. Consider this in your plans and have a backup option or shelter available to ensure a delightful experience for all.

Engage with local professionals who have a deep understanding of the regional climate. Local vendors, photographers, or wedding planners can offer valuable insights into the typical weather patterns of your chosen location. Their expertise becomes an invaluable resource, guiding you in making informed decisions and adapting your plans to suit the atmospheric nuances of the region.

Remember that flexibility is key when adapting plans based on regional climates. Nature, with its inherent unpredictability, may present delightful surprises or unexpected challenges. Embrace the spirit of adaptability, and view any adjustments as opportunities to enhance the uniqueness of your celebration. By aligning your plans with the regional climate, you not only ensure a seamless experience but also create a celebration that feels organically connected to the beautiful natural surroundings of your chosen location.

As you navigate the regional climates, envision a celebration that not only complements the atmospheric charm of the region but also becomes a harmonious and unforgettable chapter in the story of your love. So, with curiosity and a willingness to adapt, venture into the heart of the regional climate, where the beauty of nature intertwines with the magic of your elopement, creating memories that will last a lifetime.

Backup Plans for Unpredictable Weather

As you embark on the exhilarating journey of planning your outdoor elopement, it's wise to prepare for the unexpected twists that weather may bring. Mother Nature, with her capricious temperament, can add an element of spontaneity to your celebration. While envisioning clear skies and perfect weather is part of the joy, having backup plans in place ensures that your love story unfolds seamlessly, rain or shine.

Consider your backup plan as the understudy waiting in the wings, ready to step into the spotlight if the weather takes an unexpected turn. It's not about expecting the worst but rather about embracing the possibility of a different, equally enchanting scenario.

For ceremonies planned in open spaces, having a backup location offers shelter and peace of mind. This could be an indoor venue nearby, a charming pavilion, or even a covered gazebo. By identifying and securing a backup location in advance, you ensure that your celebration can proceed smoothly, regardless of rain, wind, or other unexpected weather challenges.

Tents, with their versatility, become valuable allies in the quest for weather-proof celebrations. Consider having an elegant tent as part of your original plan or as a backup option. Tents not only provide shelter but also create a cozy and intimate atmosphere for your celebration. They can be adorned with lights, drapes, and decorations, transforming them into enchanting spaces that seamlessly blend with the outdoors.

Another charming backup option is to embrace the weather itself. If rain decides to make an appearance, consider incorporating stylish umbrellas into your ceremony. This not only adds a whimsical touch to your celebration but also allows you to dance with the raindrops, creating memorable and unique moments. Embracing the elements can turn an unexpected weather challenge into an opportunity for creativity and spontaneity.

Engage with your photographer and other vendors to discuss and plan for potential weather-related scenarios. A skilled photographer can capture the beauty of your celebration, rain or shine. Work together to identify picturesque spots that can serve as backdrops in various weather conditions. Having a collaborative approach with your vendors ensures that everyone is on the same page and ready to adapt to changing weather dynamics.

Flexibility is the golden key to navigating unpredictable weather. Embrace the idea that your celebration might take a slightly different course than initially planned, and trust that the adaptability of your backup plans will lead to beautiful and unexpected moments. Keep an open mind, and view any changes as part of the unique story of your elopement.

Ultimately, your outdoor elopement is a celebration of love, connection, and the beauty of nature. By having backup plans in place, you're not just prepared for weather variations but also for the opportunity to create a celebration that is resilient, spontaneous, and filled with the magic of the unexpected. So, as you weave your backup plans into the tapestry of your elopement preparations, envision a celebration that unfolds gracefully, embracing every element and weathering any storm with the strength and beauty of enduring love.

Developing flexible contingency plans

In the intricate dance of planning an outdoor elopement, flexibility emerges as a delightful dance partner, ready to twirl gracefully when unpredictable weather takes center stage. Developing flexible contingency plans becomes the choreography that ensures your celebration remains a seamless performance, no matter the atmospheric twists.

Think of flexible contingency plans as the choreographed steps that adapt to the rhythm of the weather. These plans allow you to gracefully transition from an outdoor ceremony to an indoor setting, a tented space, or even an alternative scenic location. By having a spectrum of options that align with your original vision, you maintain the essence of your love story while accommodating the unpredictable nuances of nature.

Engage with your venue or local vendors to explore the possibilities for flexible indoor alternatives. This could be a charming nearby venue, a cozy indoor space with large windows offering scenic views, or an elegant pavilion that seamlessly integrates with the outdoors. Developing relationships with local venues and vendors allows you to tap into their expertise, ensuring that your flexible contingency plans align seamlessly with the charm of your chosen location.

Consider incorporating tents into your contingency plans. Tents, with their versatility, offer a graceful transition between indoor and outdoor settings. Whether it's an open-sided tent that allows the beauty of nature to shine through or a fully enclosed tent providing shelter from the elements, these temporary structures become flexible canvases that adapt to the changing weather while preserving the enchantment of your celebration.

Explore the magic of spontaneity by having flexible ceremony spaces that can be easily rearranged or adapted based on weather conditions. This could involve having multiple ceremony setups, each designed for a specific weather scenario. For instance, consider a layout that allows for a quick transition from an open-air ceremony to a covered space if rain unexpectedly graces your celebration.

Collaborate with your vendors, especially your photographer and florist, to develop flexible contingency plans that enhance the visual story of your elopement. Discuss alternative photo locations, adaptable floral arrangements, and creative ways to embrace the unexpected. A collaborative approach ensures that every detail of your celebration, from decor to photography, aligns seamlessly with the flexible contingency plans in place.

Communicate openly with your guests about the possibility of changes to the original plan. By setting expectations and fostering an atmosphere of flexibility, you create a supportive environment where everyone can embrace the beauty of spontaneity. Encourage your loved ones to appreciate the unfolding story of your celebration, knowing that every twist in the weather adds a unique chapter to the narrative.

As you develop flexible contingency plans, envision a celebration that not only weathers the unpredictability of nature but also dances gracefully with each unexpected turn. Your love story, with its twists and turns, becomes a testament to resilience, adaptability, and the enduring beauty of connection. So, as you embrace the art of flexibility in your elopement planning, picture a celebration that unfolds with the fluidity and elegance of a perfectly choreographed dance, leaving you with cherished memories that withstand the test of time.

Tips for staying prepared without sacrificing the adventure

Navigating the unpredictable nature of weather during your outdoor elopement is akin to embarking on a thrilling adventure. Staying prepared without sacrificing the spirit of spontaneity adds an extra layer of excitement to your celebration. Here are some tips to ensure you're ready for the unexpected while embracing the adventurous essence of your elopement.

First and foremost, keep an eye on the weather forecast. While nature might surprise you, having a general idea of what to expect allows you to make informed decisions. Check the forecast leading up to your celebration and on the day itself, considering the timing of potential weather changes. This knowledge becomes your compass, guiding you through the atmospheric landscapes of your elopement.

When it comes to attire, opt for flexibility and layers. Choosing clothing that can easily adapt to changing weather conditions ensures you stay comfortable and stylish throughout the day. If there's a chance of rain, consider elegant waterproof options like a chic rain jacket or a transparent umbrella that adds a touch of romance to the proceedings. Embrace the idea that your attire can be both practical and enchanting, adapting seamlessly to the whims of nature.

Select a hairstyle that can withstand various weather scenarios. If rain is a possibility, opt for styles that are less likely to be affected by moisture. Consult with your hairstylist about weather-resistant products and hairstyles that complement the potential atmospheric conditions. By being proactive, you ensure that your look remains polished and picture-perfect, rain or shine.

Consider the timing of your elopement ceremony. Being mindful of the weather patterns at different times of the day allows you to strategically plan your celebration. If there's a chance of rain, scheduling your ceremony during a period of lower precipitation can increase the likelihood of a dry and delightful experience. Similarly, if you're seeking a warm and sunlit celebration, timing your ceremony during the sunniest hours enhances the luminous atmosphere.

Engage with local professionals who understand the unique weather patterns of your chosen location. Local vendors, photographers, or wedding planners can offer valuable insights and tips based on their experience with the regional climate. Their expertise becomes an invaluable resource, helping you make decisions that align with the atmospheric charm of your elopement.

Create a weather emergency kit that includes essentials like umbrellas, blankets, and any other items that might come in handy based on the expected weather conditions. This kit becomes your treasure chest of practical solutions, ensuring you're equipped to handle unexpected weather twists without compromising the magic of the moment.

Be open to the idea of spontaneous changes. Embrace the adventure that comes with the unpredictability of weather, knowing that every unexpected turn adds a unique chapter to your love story. Allow the serendipity of nature to shape your celebration, creating memories that are infused with the warmth of connection and the beauty of spontaneity.

Ultimately, staying prepared without sacrificing the adventure is about finding the delicate balance between planning and embracing the unknown. As you weave these tips into the fabric of your elopement preparations, envision a celebration that unfolds with the spirit of a grand adventure, where every weather-related surprise becomes a cherished part of the story you'll tell for years to come. So, with a spirit of curiosity and preparedness, venture into the heart of your outdoor elopement, ready for whatever atmospheric wonders nature may unveil.

Embracing the Elements

In the grand tapestry of your outdoor elopement, the elements play a pivotal role, each raindrop, gust of wind, and ray of sunshine contributing to the unique story of your celebration. Embracing the elements becomes a dance with nature, an invitation to intertwine your love story with the ever-changing rhythms of the environment.

Picture this chapter as an ode to the elements, celebrating the wind that whispers through the trees, the raindrops that add a poetic rhythm to your vows, and the sun that bathes your celebration in a warm glow. Embracing the elements isn't just about weathering the storm; it's about inviting nature to become an integral part of the narrative of your love.

For those who find themselves exchanging vows under a gentle rain shower, consider it a blessing from the heavens. Rain, with its rhythmic patter, adds a symphony of nature to your celebration. Embrace the idea of dancing in the rain, allowing each drop to become a note in the love song you're composing.

Elegant umbrellas, stylish rain boots, and the sparkle of raindrops on leaves create a whimsical and enchanting atmosphere.

Wind, with its playful spirit, can add a touch of drama to your elopement. Imagine your veil gently billowing in the breeze as you say your vows, or the rustle of leaves providing a natural soundtrack to your ceremony. Consider incorporating wind-friendly elements into your decor, such as flowing fabrics or delicate wind chimes. Embracing the wind becomes a poetic dance, adding an ethereal quality to your celebration.

Sunshine, with its golden embrace, paints your celebration in a warm and radiant glow. Bask in the sunlight as you exchange vows, and let the natural beauty of your surroundings shine brightly. Consider choosing outdoor locations that capture the best of the sunlight, creating a luminous and joyous atmosphere. Embracing the sunshine is an invitation to revel in the warmth and brightness of your love.

If your celebration unfolds amidst the snow-covered landscapes of winter, embrace the serene beauty of the elements. Picture saying your vows against a backdrop of glistening snow, the hushed stillness of winter creating an intimate and enchanting atmosphere. Cozy blankets, warm attire, and the crisp beauty of a winter wonderland become integral elements in this seasonal celebration.

Engage with your photographer to capture the magic of the elements. A skilled photographer can turn raindrops into diamonds, wind into a playful dance, and sunshine into a golden embrace. By embracing the elements in your photos, you immortalize the atmospheric charm of your elopement, creating a visual story that beautifully weaves together nature and love.

Consider incorporating natural elements into your decor that harmonize with the surroundings. From earthy florals to eco-friendly materials, let the decor reflect the beauty of the elements. This not only enhances the visual appeal of your celebration but also fosters a connection between your love story and the natural world.

As you embark on the journey of embracing the elements, envision a celebration that transcends the traditional boundaries of weather and becomes a symphony of nature and love. Let the raindrops, the wind, the sunshine, or the snow become participants in your love story, adding depth, texture, and a touch of magic to every moment. So, with open hearts and a willingness to dance with nature, step into the embrace of the elements, creating memories that resonate with the timeless beauty of your extraordinary love.

Incorporating weather into the ceremony's atmosphere

Incorporating the weather into your elopement ceremony transforms nature's whims into a magical dance that elevates the atmosphere of your celebration. Rather than seeing rain, wind, sunshine, or snow as mere elements, consider them as enchanting co-stars in the love story you're about to unfold. This approach not only adds a unique and memorable dimension to your ceremony but also fosters a deeper connection between your love and the natural world.

Let's begin with the romantic patter of raindrops. If your celebration is graced by a gentle shower, consider making it an integral part of the ceremony's ambiance. Imagine saying your vows under a canopy of umbrellas, each raindrop contributing a soft melody to the poetic soundtrack of your love story. Encourage your guests to embrace the rain, providing elegant umbrellas as both practical and stylish accessories. The scent of rain-soaked earth and the gentle sound of droplets on leaves become harmonious elements that infuse your ceremony with an ethereal and enchanting quality.

Wind, with its playful spirit, can be invited to dance alongside you during the ceremony. Picture the gentle rustling of leaves or the billowing of fabric decor in response to the wind's whims. Consider incorporating wind chimes or delicate ribbons into your ceremony setup, allowing the wind to weave its own choreography into the celebration. Embracing the wind becomes a poetic acknowledgment of the ever-changing and unpredictable nature of love.

For those who choose to exchange vows under the warm embrace of sunshine, let the golden rays become an integral part of your ceremony's atmosphere. Position your ceremony space to capture the best of the sunlight, creating a luminous and joyous ambiance. Consider elements like sunflowers in your decor or gold accents that mirror the brilliance of the sun. The warmth of the sunlight not only bathes your celebration in a radiant glow but also adds a tangible and uplifting energy to the ceremony.

Winter elopements, adorned in the serene beauty of snow, offer a blank canvas for creating a magical atmosphere. Picture saying your vows against a backdrop of glistening snow, with each snowflake adding a touch of enchantment to the ceremony. Embrace the elements with cozy blankets, perhaps a fur stole, and seasonal decor that complements the winter wonderland. The hushed stillness of snowfall becomes a serene backdrop, creating a tranquil and intimate atmosphere for your vows.

Engaging with your photographer becomes a crucial aspect of incorporating weather into the ceremony's atmosphere. A skilled photographer can capture the beauty of raindrops, the playfulness of the wind, the warmth of sunlight, or the magical stillness of snow in a way that immortalizes these atmospheric elements as an essential part of your love story. Work collaboratively to create a visual narrative that seamlessly intertwines the natural world with your celebration.

When incorporating weather into the ceremony's atmosphere, communicate openly with your guests about the elements. Encourage them to embrace the unpredictability and spontaneity that weather can bring, creating an atmosphere of shared adventure and connection. Provide practical items like blankets or fans, depending on the weather, ensuring everyone remains comfortable and engaged in the atmospheric beauty of the ceremony.

As you exchange vows in the midst of the elements, envision a ceremony that becomes a symphony of nature and love. Let the weather weave its own story, adding layers of depth, emotion, and magic to the moments you'll cherish forever. So, with a spirit of openness and a willingness to dance with the elements, step into the ceremony where nature becomes an active participant, contributing to the timeless and atmospheric beauty of your extraordinary love.

Choosing attire and decor that complements outdoor conditions

Selecting attire and decor that harmonizes with outdoor conditions is a thoughtful and practical approach to ensure both comfort and style during your elopement. Rather than viewing the elements as potential challenges, consider them as inspiring cues for creating an atmosphere that seamlessly blends with the natural surroundings.

Let's begin with attire. For a rainy celebration, embrace the opportunity to don elegant and weather-appropriate attire. Consider a stylish rain jacket or a transparent umbrella that not only shields you from the rain but also adds a touch of romance to your ensemble. Opt for waterproof footwear, ensuring your feet stay dry and comfortable as you navigate rain-kissed landscapes. Embracing the rain with purposeful attire not only showcases your adaptability but also transforms potential challenges into stylish and memorable moments.

In windy conditions, choose attire that complements the playful spirit of the wind. Flowing fabrics, such as a lightweight and ethereal wedding dress, create a dynamic and graceful effect as they respond to the wind's movements. Secure hairstyles with wind-resistant styles, allowing you to move freely without worrying about tresses being tousled. By selecting attire that dances with the wind rather than against it, you not only enhance the visual appeal but also embrace the natural rhythm of the environment.

Sunlit celebrations call for attire that reflects the warmth and radiance of the sunlight. Consider lightweight fabrics, breathable designs, and open-back dresses that allow you to bask in the sun's embrace. Opt for lighter colors that complement the brightness of the surroundings, creating a luminous and joyful atmosphere. Sun hats and sunglasses become both stylish accessories and practical elements, adding a touch of flair to your ensemble while ensuring you stay comfortable under the sunlight.

For winter elopements, embrace attire that not only provides warmth but also complements the serene beauty of snow-covered landscapes. Cozy shawls, fur stoles, or even a chic winter jacket can be stylish additions to your ensemble, offering both comfort and seasonal charm. Select footwear that is not only fashionable but also suitable for walking in snow, ensuring you move with ease and grace in the winter wonderland. The key is to blend practicality with style, creating an ensemble that not only shields you from the elements but also enhances the overall aesthetic of your celebration.

When it comes to decor, choose elements that seamlessly integrate with the outdoor conditions. For rainy celebrations, consider waterproof or water-resistant decor that can withstand the rain without losing its charm. Fabric drapes that sway gracefully in the wind, or floral arrangements that incorporate weather-resistant blooms, become enchanting additions to windy elopements. Sunlit celebrations allow for the use of natural elements like sunflowers, warm-colored florals, and decor that captures the essence of the season.

Winter elopements provide a canvas of snow, allowing you to create a magical atmosphere with decor that complements the serene beauty of the surroundings. Consider evergreen branches, frosted decor, and seasonal elements that harmonize with the winter landscape. By selecting decor that aligns with the outdoor conditions, you not only enhance the visual appeal but also create a cohesive and atmospheric celebration.

Engage with your photographer to capture the unique charm of your chosen attire and decor in the context of the outdoor conditions. A skilled photographer can weave the elements seamlessly into the visual narrative of your celebration, creating a series of images that showcase the beauty of adaptability and the harmony between nature and style.

As you choose attire and decor that complements outdoor conditions, envision a celebration where every element, from the fabric of your dress to the flowers in your bouquet, becomes an integral part of the atmospheric story. By embracing the outdoors in your ensemble and decor choices, you not only ensure practicality and comfort but also elevate the aesthetic of your elopement, creating a celebration that resonates with the timeless beauty of love in harmony with nature. So, with an eye for style and a spirit of adaptability, step into your elopement dressed in a way that celebrates both your love and the enchanting elements that surround you.

Chapter 4: Crafting an Adventure-Packed Itinerary

Welcome to Chapter 4: Crafting an Adventure-Packed Itinerary—an exhilarating journey that transforms your elopement into a seamless blend of love and adventure. In this chapter, we embark on the exciting task of curating a schedule that not only celebrates your union but also infuses the spirit of exploration and joy into every moment.

Your elopement is not just a ceremony; it's an adventure, a grand expedition into the heart of love and connection. Crafting an adventure-packed itinerary is about more than scheduling; it's about creating a dynamic and unforgettable experience that mirrors the unique essence of your relationship.

Imagine a day filled with not just vows and rings but also with laughter, discovery, and shared adventures. From the quiet serenity of a sunrise ceremony to the thrill of exploring scenic landscapes hand in hand, this chapter guides you in choreographing a day that unfolds like a captivating story—a story written by love, adorned with the beauty of nature, and punctuated by moments of shared joy.

We'll explore how to seamlessly blend the practical aspects of your elopement, like the ceremony and photography sessions, with exciting and personalized adventures. Whether it's hiking to a breathtaking viewpoint, enjoying a picnic in a secluded meadow, or dancing under the stars, your itinerary becomes a canvas for painting a day that is as unique as your love story.

This chapter is a compass, guiding you through the process of designing an itinerary that aligns with your passions, showcases your personalities, and leaves room for spontaneity. Adventure isn't just about grand gestures; it's about finding joy in the little moments, reveling in the shared experiences that make your elopement an extraordinary and intimate celebration.

So, let's dive into the art of crafting an adventure-packed itinerary—a chapter that unfolds with the excitement of a treasure hunt, where each planned moment and unexpected discovery become precious gems in the tapestry of your love. As you turn the pages, envision a day that not only marks the beginning of your married life but also stands as a testament to the adventurous spirit that fuels your journey together.

Pre-Wedding Adventures

Before the vows are exchanged and the rings are placed, the stage is set with the pre-wedding adventures—a delightful overture to the main performance of your elopement day. This chapter explores the art of crafting pre-wedding adventures that add a touch of excitement, joy, and shared experiences to the moments leading up to your ceremony.

Picture this: the morning sun painting the sky in hues of pink and gold as you embark on a leisurely hike together. The rustle of leaves, the scent of nature awakening, and the anticipation of the day ahead create a tranquil yet invigorating atmosphere. Pre-wedding adventures are the canvas on which you paint the initial strokes of your elopement day, setting the tone for a celebration that is both intimate and adventurous.

Consider starting your pre-wedding adventures with a sunrise activity, be it a scenic hike, a tranquil yoga session, or a leisurely stroll along the beach. The magic of the early morning light not only adds a romantic glow to your experiences but also provides a serene backdrop for quiet moments of reflection and connection.

Engage in activities that resonate with your shared interests and passions. Whether it's exploring a local market, sharing a cup of coffee at a charming café, or indulging in a favorite hobby, pre-wedding adventures become a canvas for creating memories that reflect the uniqueness of your relationship. These shared moments not only enhance the bond between you but also infuse your elopement day with a personalized touch.

Incorporate elements of surprise into your pre-wedding adventures. Perhaps a scenic helicopter ride, a hot air balloon excursion, or a spontaneous detour to a hidden gem in the area. These unexpected twists not only add an element of excitement but also create stories that will be recounted with joy in the years to come.

Capture the essence of your pre-wedding adventures through photography. A skilled photographer can immortalize the candid moments, the laughter, and the shared glances, creating a visual narrative that beautifully encapsulates the anticipation and joy of the moments leading up to your ceremony. These photos become cherished mementos, capturing the spirit of your pre-wedding adventures in a way that words cannot express.

As you craft your pre-wedding adventures, let spontaneity be your guide. Embrace the joy of discovering hidden gems, the thrill of trying something new together, and the beauty of being fully present in the moment. Pre-wedding adventures are not just about the activities themselves but about the connection they foster and the memories they create— a tapestry of shared experiences that will forever be woven into the fabric of your love story.

So, envision a morning filled with laughter, discovery, and shared adventures, setting the stage for the main act of your elopement day. As you engage in pre-wedding adventures, let each moment be a brushstroke on the canvas of your love, creating a masterpiece that is as unique and extraordinary as the journey you are about to embark on together.

Planning outdoor activities leading up to the ceremony

In the intricate dance of planning pre-wedding adventures, the art of orchestrating outdoor activities leading up to the ceremony emerges as a captivating overture—a series of moments that build anticipation, create lasting memories, and infuse the air with the joy of shared experiences. This section delves into the nuances of planning outdoor activities, ensuring that each chosen endeavor becomes a delightful brushstroke on the canvas of your elopement day.

Consider the natural beauty of the surroundings as the backdrop for your pre-ceremony outdoor activities. Whether you're surrounded by lush greenery, pristine beaches, or majestic mountain landscapes, let the outdoor setting set the stage for the adventures that will unfold. The charm of nature becomes an integral part of the experience, creating a seamless connection between your activities and the environment.

Engage in activities that not only reflect your interests but also complement the overall vibe of your elopement. If you share a love for adventure, consider a morning hike to a scenic viewpoint or a kayaking excursion on a tranquil lake. For those who appreciate a more relaxed pace, a leisurely bike ride through charming trails or a picnic in a serene meadow can be the perfect prelude to your ceremony. By aligning the activities with your personalities, you ensure that each moment is a true reflection of your unique connection.

Incorporate elements of romance into your outdoor activities, building a sense of intimacy that sets the tone for the upcoming ceremony. A quiet stroll along a moonlit beach, a cozy blanket laid out under the stars, or a shared moment watching the sunrise—all contribute to the romantic atmosphere that defines the essence of an elopement. These activities become not just adventures but love-infused experiences that deepen the connection between you.

Plan activities that allow for moments of reflection and quiet connection. Amidst the excitement and joy, provide opportunities for you and your partner to share intimate conversations, exchange glances filled with anticipation, and revel in the quiet beauty of the natural surroundings. These contemplative moments become the emotional undercurrents that add depth to the overall experience, creating a nuanced and memorable narrative.

Consider the logistics of the outdoor activities, ensuring that they seamlessly flow into the next elements of your elopement day. From the location of the activities to the timing and transportation, thoughtful planning ensures a smooth transition from each adventure to the next. This cohesive approach allows you to savor each moment without the distraction of logistical concerns, creating a seamless and enjoyable experience for both you and your guests.

Capture the magic of these outdoor activities through photography. A skilled photographer can weave the essence of each adventure into a visual narrative that beautifully encapsulates the joy, anticipation, and connection of the moments leading up to the ceremony. These photographs become not just snapshots but timeless mementos that vividly evoke the spirit of your pre-ceremony outdoor activities.

As you plan these activities, envision a sequence of adventures that build upon each other, creating a crescendo of excitement and joy. Let the natural beauty, shared interests, and romantic undertones guide your choices, ensuring that each outdoor activity becomes a meaningful and cherished chapter in the story of your elopement. So, with a spirit of adventure and a heart filled with anticipation, step into the outdoor activities that lead you toward the main act of your extraordinary celebration.

Bonding experiences for the couple and select guests

In the mosaic of pre-wedding adventures, the notion of crafting bonding experiences for the couple and select guests emerges as a heartwarming melody—a symphony of shared moments that deepen connections, create memories, and foster an intimate atmosphere leading up to the ceremony. This section explores the art of curating bonding experiences that transcend the ordinary, inviting you and your chosen guests to engage in activities that strengthen the ties of friendship and family.

Consider these bonding experiences as a tapestry of shared joy, woven from threads of laughter, shared stories, and the collective spirit of celebration. As the couple, these moments allow you to not only connect with each other on a deeper level but also to create bonds with the select guests who are part of this intimate journey.

Engage in activities that encourage collaboration and teamwork. Whether it's a group cooking class, a creative art session, or a team-building outdoor adventure, these experiences provide a shared platform for everyone to contribute, learn, and bond. The collaborative nature of these activities fosters a sense of unity, creating a harmonious atmosphere that extends beyond the individual connections.

Craft experiences that allow for meaningful conversations and shared reflections. A fireside chat under the stars, a scenic boat ride where stories flow as freely as the water, or a cozy gathering around a table filled with shared meals—these moments become the canvas on which connections deepen and memories are etched. Provide opportunities for open and heartfelt conversations, allowing everyone to share in the anticipation and joy of the impending ceremony.

Incorporate elements of surprise and spontaneity into these bonding experiences. Perhaps a surprise guest appearance, a spontaneous dance party, or a heartfelt toast that catches everyone off guard. These unexpected moments not only add an element of excitement but also contribute to the organic and genuine nature of the bonding experiences. The element of surprise becomes a shared joy that unites everyone in the celebration.

Consider the preferences and personalities of the select guests when planning these bonding experiences. Tailoring activities to align with their interests ensures that everyone feels included and engaged. Whether it's a wine tasting for the oenophiles, a nature walk for the outdoorsy, or a craft workshop for the creatively inclined, these personalized experiences create a sense of thoughtfulness and consideration.

Capture the essence of these bonding experiences through photography. A skilled photographer can immortalize the laughter, the shared glances, and the genuine connections that unfold during these moments. These photographs become not just images but tangible reminders of the bonds forged in the lead-up to the ceremony, creating a visual narrative that reflects the warmth and camaraderie of your intimate gathering.

As you curate bonding experiences, envision a series of moments where connections are deepened, laughter is shared, and the anticipation of the ceremony becomes a collective joy. Let the experiences reflect the diverse personalities and relationships within the group, creating a mosaic of memories that will be cherished by both the couple and their select guests. So, with a spirit of inclusivity and a heart open to connection, step into these bonding experiences that become a prelude to the main act of your extraordinary celebration.

The Ceremony and Beyond

As the sun sets on the canvas of pre-wedding adventures, we step into the heart of your elopement story—The Ceremony and Beyond. This section is a poetic exploration of the transformative moments that unfold as you exchange vows, rings, and promises, marking the official union of your hearts. But it doesn't end there; it extends into the afterglow of the ceremony, where the magic continues to blossom, creating a tapestry of love that lingers in the air.

The Ceremony is the centerpiece of your elopement, the moment where time seems to stand still, and the world fades away, leaving only the two of you in a cocoon of love. Whether under the open sky, surrounded by towering trees, or by the rhythmic lull of the ocean waves, the ceremony becomes a sacred space where your love is both witnessed and celebrated by nature itself.

Craft a ceremony that reflects the essence of your relationship, incorporating rituals, readings, and vows that resonate with your hearts. It's not just about the words spoken but the emotions that ripple through each promise—a symphony of love, commitment, and the shared dreams that bind you together. Whether it's an intimate exchange or a grand declaration, the ceremony becomes the canvas on which your love story is painted with the brushstrokes of authenticity.

As you exchange vows and rings, the transition into the Beyond unfolds. It's the post-ceremony moments—the quiet walk as a married couple, the stolen glances, the shared laughter, and the shared embrace—that extend the enchantment of the ceremony. The Beyond is where the intimacy of your connection is magnified, and the celebration of love takes on a more personal and nuanced tone.

Consider incorporating symbolic gestures into the Beyond—whether it's releasing butterflies, planting a sapling together, or creating a time capsule. These gestures become tangible reminders of the commitment made during the ceremony, adding layers of meaning and significance to the post-ceremony moments.

Engage in activities that deepen the sense of connection during the Beyond. Whether it's a private picnic for two, a romantic boat ride, or a scenic hike, these moments become the punctuation marks in the narrative of your elopement day. The Beyond is not just about the physical journey; it's about the emotional and spiritual exploration of the shared path ahead.

Capture the magic of the Ceremony and Beyond through photography. A skilled photographer can weave the emotions, the stolen glances, and the sheer joy of these moments into a visual tapestry that immortalizes the essence of your elopement. These photographs become more than images; they are portals to the emotions, the love, and the magic that unfolded in the sacred space of your ceremony and extended into the Beyond.

As you step into The Ceremony and Beyond, envision a journey that transcends the ordinary—a celebration that continues to unfold, blossom, and evolve with each passing moment. The Ceremony is the pivotal point, the axis on which the magic spins, and the Beyond is the ongoing chapter, the adventure that stretches into the horizon of your shared life. So, with hearts full of love and eyes set on the journey ahead, step into The Ceremony and Beyond—a timeless exploration of the extraordinary love that defines your union.

Designing a memorable outdoor ceremony

Designing a memorable outdoor ceremony is an art that transforms the natural canvas of your chosen location into a sacred space where vows are exchanged, promises are made, and the beauty of nature becomes an integral part of your union. In this section, we explore the elements that contribute to crafting an unforgettable ceremony—a moment where the outdoors not only serves as a backdrop but as a co-creator of the magic that unfolds.

Start by considering the unique features of the outdoor setting. Whether it's the rustling leaves in a forest, the rhythmic waves of the ocean, or the panoramic views from a mountain summit, let the natural elements guide the design of your ceremony. Position yourselves in a way that allows the landscape to become an active participant, framing the ceremony with the breathtaking beauty of nature.

Incorporate meaningful rituals that resonate with both of you and the outdoor setting. Whether it's a unity ceremony involving elements from nature, the planting of a symbolic tree, or the release of biodegradable confetti, these rituals become a poetic expression of your love story intertwined with the elements around you. The ceremony becomes a dance between human connection and the natural world.

Choose decor that complements rather than competes with the outdoor surroundings. Consider elements like floral arrangements that mirror the local flora, aisle runners made of natural materials, or simple yet elegant arches that frame the ceremony space. Let the decor enhance the natural beauty without overshadowing it, creating a harmonious visual experience for both you and your guests.

Embrace the spontaneity of the outdoors. Whether it's a gentle breeze, the warmth of sunlight filtering through the leaves, or the sound of birdsong, allow these natural elements to become an integral part of the ceremony. A strategically placed wind chime or the rustling of leaves can add a symphonic quality to the proceedings, creating a sensorial experience that transcends the visual.

Consider the logistics of an outdoor ceremony, ensuring that everyone can comfortably witness and participate. Provide shade or seating as needed, have a backup plan for unexpected weather changes, and consider the comfort of both the couple and the guests. A well-thought-out plan ensures that everyone can fully immerse themselves in the beauty of the ceremony without any logistical distractions.

Engage the senses during the ceremony. Consider incorporating elements like fragrant flowers, the sound of a babbling brook, or the feel of natural textures in the decor. Creating a sensory-rich experience allows everyone to be fully present in the moment, heightening the emotional impact of the ceremony.

Capture the essence of the outdoor ceremony through photography. A skilled photographer can immortalize the landscape, the emotions, and the intimate moments, creating a visual narrative that transports you back to the sacred space of your vows. These photographs become not just memories but portals to the magic that unfolded in the heart of nature.

As you design a memorable outdoor ceremony, envision it as a collaboration between your love story and the natural world. Let the surroundings inspire the elements of the ceremony, creating a tapestry of moments that reflect the unique beauty of your union. The outdoors becomes not just a setting but an active participant, contributing to the timeless and unforgettable experience of your elopement ceremony. So, with reverence for nature and hearts full of love, step into the designed masterpiece that is your outdoor ceremony—a moment that transcends time and becomes an eternal part of your shared journey.

Transitioning into post-ceremony adventures and celebrations

As the echoes of vows exchanged and promises made linger in the air, the transition into post-ceremony adventures and celebrations marks the unfolding of a new chapter—an exhilarating continuation of your elopement day. This section explores the art of seamlessly moving from the sacred space of the ceremony into the joyous realm of shared adventures and celebrations, creating a dynamic and harmonious flow that mirrors the rhythm of your love story.

Consider the post-ceremony moments as a bridge between the sacred and the celebratory—a time where the emotions of the ceremony still resonate, and the anticipation for what lies ahead builds. The transition becomes a gentle dance, guided by the shared energy of the couple and the intimate gathering of select guests.

Engage in a symbolic act that marks the transition. Whether it's a shared toast, a group hug, or a spontaneous dance, these moments become the punctuation marks that signify the shift from the formality of the ceremony to the lightheartedness of the post-ceremony adventures. The transition is not just a physical journey but a collective emotional shift that sets the stage for what's to come.

Plan post-ceremony adventures that reflect the spirit of your relationship and the natural setting. Whether it's a scenic hike to a breathtaking viewpoint, a leisurely stroll along the beach, or a picnic in a picturesque meadow, these adventures become an extension of the ceremony, allowing the couple and select guests to continue basking in the beauty of the outdoors. The adventures become not just activities but shared experiences that deepen connections and create lasting memories.

Consider the logistics of the transition, ensuring a smooth flow from the ceremony site to the location of post-ceremony adventures. Provide clear directions, arrange for transportation if needed, and ensure that everyone feels comfortable and included in the plans. A well-executed transition allows everyone to focus on the joy of the moment without the distraction of logistical concerns.

Incorporate surprise elements into the post-ceremony adventures. Whether it's a hidden treasure hunt, a surprise musical performance, or a spontaneous detour to a scenic spot, these unexpected twists add an element of excitement and create memories that will be recounted with joy in the years to come. The surprises become the spontaneous notes in the symphony of your elopement day.

Capture the energy and joy of the post-ceremony adventures through photography. A skilled photographer can immortalize the laughter, the shared glances, and the sheer joy of these moments, creating a visual narrative that beautifully encapsulates the spirit of the post-ceremony celebrations. These photographs become not just snapshots but cherished mementos that vividly evoke the atmosphere of shared joy and adventure.

As you transition into post-ceremony adventures and celebrations, envision it as a continuation of the love story—a dynamic and unfolding chapter that mirrors the essence of your relationship. The adventures become the strokes on the canvas of your elopement day, creating a tapestry of experiences that seamlessly blend the sacred with the celebratory. So, with hearts full of anticipation and a spirit of adventure, step into the post-ceremony realm—an extraordinary continuation of the extraordinary celebration that is your elopement day.

Balancing Adventure and Intimacy

In the delicate dance of planning an elopement, the art of balancing adventure and intimacy emerges as a crucial element—a harmonious interplay that ensures your celebration is both thrilling and deeply personal. This section explores the nuanced approach of weaving moments of adventure seamlessly into the fabric of intimate experiences, creating a celebration that resonates with the unique dynamics of your relationship.

Start by considering the shared interests and passions that define your relationship. Whether it's a love for hiking, a passion for exploring new cuisines, or an appreciation for art, these interests become the foundation upon which you build the adventure. Choose activities that not only excite you but also deepen the connection between you and your partner, creating a tapestry of shared experiences that reflect the essence of your love story.

Tailor the level of adventure to align with your comfort zones. Whether you're avid adventurers seeking a thrilling escapade or prefer a more relaxed pace, the key is to find a balance that resonates with both of you. The adventure becomes a means of enhancing the celebration, adding an extra layer of joy and excitement without overshadowing the intimate moments.

Incorporate elements of surprise into the adventure. Whether it's a spontaneous detour to a hidden gem, a surprise activity that catches you off guard, or an unexpected twist in the itinerary, these surprises become the spontaneous notes that elevate the sense of adventure. The element of surprise adds a delightful touch, creating memories that are etched with spontaneity and joy.

Create moments of intimacy within the adventure. Whether it's a quiet picnic in a scenic spot, a shared moment watching the sunset, or a cozy campfire under the stars, these pockets of intimacy become the emotional anchors that ground the adventure in the warmth of connection. The adventure is not just about the external experiences but about the internal journey of shared moments and emotions.

Consider the logistics of the adventure, ensuring that it complements the overall flow of the elopement day. Whether it's the timing of the adventure, transportation arrangements, or the integration of adventure into the post-ceremony celebrations, a thoughtful approach ensures that the adventure enhances the overall experience without creating disruptions.

Capture the essence of the adventure and intimacy through photography. A skilled photographer can immortalize the thrill of the adventure, the quiet moments of connection, and the shared joy, creating a visual narrative that beautifully encapsulates the balance between adventure and intimacy. These photographs become not just images but portals to the emotions and experiences of your elopement day.

As you navigate the delicate balance between adventure and intimacy, envision it as a dance—fluid, dynamic, and perfectly attuned to the rhythms of your relationship. Let the adventure be the backdrop against which moments of intimacy flourish, creating a celebration that is both exhilarating and deeply personal. The balance becomes the magic that defines your elopement day, a celebration where each moment, whether thrilling or tender, contributes to the extraordinary tapestry of your love story. So, with hearts open to adventure and a commitment to intimate connection, step into the harmonious dance that is your elopement—a celebration that beautifully balances the thrill of the unknown with the warmth of shared moments.

Ensuring the day remains intimate despite adventurous plans

In the grand tapestry of planning an elopement that combines adventure and intimacy, the delicate task of ensuring the day remains intimate despite adventurous plans emerges as a gentle art—a thoughtful approach that weaves moments of connection seamlessly into the fabric of excitement and exploration. This section explores the strategies and considerations that safeguard the intimacy of your celebration, ensuring that, amidst the thrill of adventure, the essence of your love story remains at the forefront.

Begin by establishing clear boundaries for the level of adventure. While seeking thrilling experiences is part of the elopement allure, understanding your comfort zones and setting clear expectations allows you to choose adventurous activities that enhance rather than overwhelm the intimate atmosphere. The adventure becomes a complementary element, adding joy without overshadowing the core of the celebration.

Select adventure activities that inherently allow for moments of intimacy. Whether it's a scenic hike that leads to a secluded spot, a hot air balloon ride with panoramic views, or a quiet canoe trip along a serene river, choose adventures that naturally create pockets of closeness. These activities become vessels for shared experiences, where the adventure becomes a backdrop to the intimacy.

Integrate moments of quiet connection into the adventure itinerary. Whether it's a pause to enjoy a quiet picnic, a moment of reflection by a scenic vista, or a shared embrace under the stars, these intentional pauses become the threads that weave the adventure seamlessly with moments of intimacy. The key is to create a rhythmic flow where adventure and connection harmoniously coexist.

Personalize the adventure by incorporating elements that hold sentimental value. Whether it's revisiting the place where you first met, incorporating shared hobbies into the adventure, or choosing a location with special meaning to both of you, these personal touches infuse the adventure with a sense of intimacy. The adventure becomes a canvas for the unique story of your relationship.

Limit the size of the group participating in the adventurous activities. Whether it's just the couple or a small group of select guests, keeping the circle intimate ensures that the adventure remains a shared experience among those closest to you. The more intimate the group, the easier it becomes to cultivate moments of connection amidst the excitement.

Communicate openly with your photographer about your vision for the day. A skilled photographer can play a pivotal role in capturing the balance between adventure and intimacy. By articulating your desires for both thrilling and tender moments, you ensure that the visual narrative of your elopement day reflects the unique blend of excitement and closeness.

Embrace spontaneity and be open to the unexpected. While planning is crucial, leaving room for unplanned moments allows for genuine connections to unfold. Whether it's a spontaneous dance in a picturesque location, an impromptu vow renewal, or a shared laugh over an unexpected twist in the adventure, these unplanned moments become the organic expressions of intimacy.

As you navigate the path of ensuring the day remains intimate despite adventurous plans, envision it as a dance of intention and spontaneity—a beautifully orchestrated balance that allows for the thrill of the unknown while preserving the sanctity of your connection. The adventure becomes not just a series of activities but a canvas upon which the colors of intimacy are vividly painted. So, with a heart attuned to both excitement and closeness, step into the adventure that is your elopement day—a celebration where the thrill of the journey is enhanced by the warmth of shared moments.

Incorporating adventure without overwhelming the celebration

In the delicate alchemy of planning an elopement, incorporating adventure without overwhelming the celebration is a nuanced art—a thoughtful navigation that ensures the thrill of the journey harmonizes with the intimacy of the moment. This section delves into the strategies and considerations that allow the adventure to gracefully weave into the celebration, enriching the experience without overshadowing the essence of your love story.

Start by defining the role of adventure within the celebration. Understand what adventure means to both of you and how it aligns with the narrative of your relationship. Whether it's an adrenaline-pumping activity, a scenic exploration, or a combination of both, clarity on the purpose of adventure becomes the compass that guides its integration into the celebration.

Choose adventure activities that naturally lend themselves to shared moments and connection. Whether it's a thrilling zip line experience, a serene hot air balloon ride, or a scenic hike to a breathtaking viewpoint, opt for activities that inherently provide opportunities for closeness. The adventure becomes a backdrop for shared experiences, allowing you and your partner to connect in the midst of excitement.

Consider the pacing of the adventure within the overall flow of the day. Integrate adventure at intervals that allow for moments of pause and reflection. Whether it's a break for a quiet picnic, a serene interlude by a scenic vista, or a moment of connection before and after the adventure, pacing ensures that the thrill of the journey unfolds in a way that complements the emotional rhythm of the celebration.

Personalize the adventure to make it meaningful and aligned with your relationship. Incorporate elements that reflect your shared interests, milestones, or inside jokes. By infusing personal touches into the adventure, it transforms from a generic activity into a tailored experience that feels deeply connected to your unique love story.

Limit the number of adventurous elements to avoid overwhelming the celebration. Instead of a series of high-intensity activities, choose a carefully curated selection that adds excitement without creating a sense of chaos. The goal is to create a balance where adventure serves as a spice, enhancing the overall flavor of the celebration without dominating the palate.

Create intentional moments of reflection and connection during the adventure. Whether it's a pause to take in a breathtaking view, a quiet exchange of words during a serene boat ride, or a shared toast in the midst of an outdoor activity, these intentional pauses become the bridges between adventure and intimacy. They allow you to savor the thrill while grounding the experience in shared connection.

Communicate openly with your photographer about your vision for incorporating adventure. A skilled photographer can capture the dynamic interplay between adventure and celebration, ensuring that the visual narrative reflects the seamless integration of excitement and intimacy. Discussing your preferences and desired moments with the photographer enhances their ability to encapsulate the essence of your unique celebration.

Embrace the unexpected and be open to spontaneity. While planning is crucial, leaving room for unplanned moments allows for genuine connections to unfold. Whether it's an impromptu dance in a scenic location, an unplanned detour that leads to an unexpected discovery, or a shared laugh over the unpredictability of the adventure, these spontaneous moments contribute to the organic flow of the celebration.

As you embark on the journey of incorporating adventure without overwhelming the celebration, envision it as a dance of balance and harmony—a celebration where the thrill of the unknown enhances the depth of your connection. The adventure becomes not just a series of activities but a vibrant thread woven into the tapestry of your elopement, creating an experience that is uniquely yours. So, with a spirit of adventure and a heart tuned to the subtleties of connection, step into the celebration that seamlessly blends the excitement of the journey with the intimacy of your shared love story.

Chapter 5: Photography and Memories

In the enchanting tale of your elopement, Chapter 5 unfolds as a treasure trove of captured moments and everlasting memories—welcome to Photography and Memories. Here, the lens becomes the storyteller, translating the whispers of your love into timeless images that will etch themselves into the canvas of your shared history. This chapter is a celebration of the artistry that transforms mere moments into cherished memories, preserving the magic of your elopement day for eternity.

Photography is more than a technical skill; it is a dance between the photographer and the unfolding narrative of your love story. As you step into this chapter, envision the photographer not just as an observer but as a co-creator, weaving emotions, landscapes, and stolen glances into a visual symphony that mirrors the depth of your connection. Each click of the shutter is a heartbeat, a testament to the unique and extraordinary love that defines your union.

The journey through Photography and Memories is a stroll down the gallery of your elopement, where each photograph is a brushstroke capturing the hues of your emotions. From the radiance in your eyes during the ceremony to the laughter shared in post-ceremony adventures, every image becomes a portal—a timeless doorway that transports you back to the sacred moments of your celebration.

As you dive into this chapter, consider photography not just as a documentation but as a storytelling medium. Your love story is a narrative, and the photographs are the prose, the poetry, and the lyrical notes that compose the melody of your union. The photographer becomes your visual bard, eloquently narrating the chapters of your elopement day with the sensitivity of an artist and the precision of a master storyteller.

Prepare to be enchanted by the power of visual storytelling. Photography and Memories is not just about freezing moments in time; it's about creating a living, breathing album that resonates with the laughter, the tears, and the sheer joy of your celebration. So, with hearts open to the artistry of visual storytelling, step into this chapter—a gallery of memories waiting to be unveiled, a testament to the extraordinary love that makes your elopement day an eternal masterpiece.

Choosing the Right Photographer

Selecting the right photographer for your elopement is a pivotal decision, akin to choosing the curator for an art exhibition that will forever adorn the walls of your memory. In this section, we delve into the nuances of this process, guiding you through the considerations that will ensure your chosen photographer not only captures moments but also crafts a visual narrative that resonates with the essence of your love story.

First and foremost, consider the style of photography that resonates with you. Do you envision your elopement album filled with candid moments, capturing the raw and unscripted emotions? Or does a more editorial and posed approach align with your vision? Some photographers specialize in a photojournalistic style, while others excel in creating beautifully composed and artistic images. Explore different portfolios and identify the style that speaks to your heart.

Personal connection is paramount. Your photographer is not just a professional documenting an event; they are a collaborator weaving your love story into visual poetry. Schedule meetings or video calls to gauge not only their technical expertise but also their ability to understand and connect with your vision. A photographer who resonates with your story will be better equipped to capture the authenticity and intimacy of your celebration.

Reviewing a photographer's portfolio is akin to flipping through the pages of their visual diary. Look for consistency in their work—do their previous projects convey a cohesive narrative? Pay attention to the emotions captured, the composition of images, and their ability to showcase the unique beauty of each celebration. A well-curated portfolio is a testament to a photographer's skill in crafting visual stories.

Don't underestimate the power of testimonials and reviews. Insights from previous clients provide a glimpse into the photographer's working style, professionalism, and ability to adapt to different scenarios. While reviewing testimonials, consider the aspects that matter most to you, whether it's their unobtrusive presence, flexibility in challenging conditions, or their knack for capturing candid moments.

Discuss the logistics of the day with your potential photographer. Communication is key, and understanding each other's expectations ensures a smooth collaboration. Clarify the timeline, the locations, and any specific shots or moments you wish to prioritize. A photographer who is well-informed about your plans will be better prepared to capture the essence of your celebration.

Ask about their approach to editing. The editing process is the painter's brushstroke that enhances the hues of your memories. Inquire about their editing style—whether it's natural and true to life, bold and vibrant, or softly muted. Ensure that their approach aligns with your aesthetic preferences and enhances the overall mood of your elopement images.

Consider the photographer's familiarity with your chosen elopement location. If possible, hire someone who is experienced with the particular venue or the type of outdoor setting you've selected. A photographer familiar with the intricacies of a location can leverage its unique features to create stunning visuals, understanding how light plays, where the best backdrops are, and how to navigate any challenges the environment may present.

Discuss the deliverables and timeline for receiving your images. Understand the photographer's process for image selection, editing, and final delivery. Knowing when you can expect to relive your elopement through the photographs allows you to plan post-celebration activities, such as creating albums or sharing images with loved ones.

Finally, trust your instincts. The right photographer is not just a skilled professional but someone with whom you feel a connection. Your elopement day is an intimate journey, and having a photographer who understands and respects your unique love story is crucial. If you feel a genuine connection and confidence in their ability to encapsulate your celebration, you've likely found the perfect visual storyteller for your elopement.

Identifying photographers experienced in outdoor settings

As you embark on the quest to choose the right photographer for your outdoor elopement, one crucial aspect comes into focus—their experience in capturing the unique beauty of nature as a backdrop. Identifying photographers with a proven track record in outdoor settings ensures that not only are they adept at navigating the challenges of natural light and landscapes, but they also possess an innate ability to seamlessly weave the surroundings into the visual narrative of your love story.

Outdoor settings present a canvas of ever-changing elements, from the soft glow of morning light to the vibrant hues of a sunset, and a skilled photographer well-versed in these nuances can transform these elements into poetic imagery. Start by perusing the portfolios of potential photographers, paying special attention to their work in outdoor environments. Look for a diverse range of locations, seasons, and weather conditions to gauge their adaptability to different settings.

Experience in outdoor photography goes beyond technical proficiency; it involves an understanding of the ebb and flow of nature. A photographer who is familiar with the intricacies of outdoor settings is better equipped to anticipate and harness the magic of fleeting moments. Whether it's the dance of leaves in the wind, the play of shadows at golden hour, or the reflections in a serene lake, their experience allows them to capture these nuances with finesse.

Consider the types of outdoor settings the photographer has worked in. If you're planning a mountaintop ceremony, a beach elopement, or a forest celebration, finding a photographer who has successfully navigated similar environments can be invaluable. Their familiarity with the challenges and opportunities specific to certain landscapes ensures a smoother workflow and enhances the overall quality of your elopement images.

Explore their ability to leverage natural light. Outdoor settings often rely heavily on the nuances of natural light, and a seasoned outdoor photographer understands how to harness its beauty. Consider how they play with light during different times of the day, whether they can capture the warmth of a sunrise, the soft glow of a cloudy day, or the dramatic shadows of a sunset. A photographer skilled in utilizing natural light will enhance the visual storytelling of your outdoor celebration.

Inquire about their strategies for unpredictable weather. Nature's whims can add an element of unpredictability to outdoor celebrations, and a seasoned photographer will have contingency plans in place. Ask about their experiences with sudden changes in weather and how they adapt to ensure that the magic of your elopement is not dampened by unexpected rain, wind, or other weather challenges.

Review testimonials and reviews from couples who had outdoor elopements. Feedback from those who've experienced the photographer's expertise in outdoor settings can provide valuable insights into their adaptability, professionalism, and ability to capture the essence of an outdoor celebration. Look for testimonials that specifically mention the photographer's prowess in working with natural elements.

Discuss their equipment and preparation for outdoor shoots. Outdoor photography often involves more than just a camera; it requires equipment and preparedness to handle different conditions. Inquire about the types of lenses they use, whether they have experience with specialized outdoor photography gear, and how they prepare for shoots in varying environments. A well-prepared photographer ensures that technical considerations do not hinder the creative process.

Consider their understanding of the flow of outdoor events. Outdoor elopements often involve movement and exploration, whether it's a hike to a scenic location, a stroll along a beach, or a meandering path through a forest. A photographer experienced in outdoor settings understands how to seamlessly integrate these movements into the visual narrative, capturing both the grandeur of the landscape and the intimate moments within it.

In conclusion, identifying photographers experienced in outdoor settings is a strategic step in ensuring that your elopement is beautifully and authentically captured. Their familiarity with the nuances of nature, adaptability to different landscapes, and ability to navigate the challenges of outdoor photography contribute to a visual storytelling experience that elevates the magic of your celebration amidst the beauty of the great outdoors.

Collaborating with photographers to capture the essence of nature

Collaborating with your chosen photographer is not just about hiring a professional to document your elopement—it's a shared journey where the photographer becomes a co-creator in capturing the essence of nature as the backdrop to your love story. In this collaborative dance, your vision, the photographer's expertise, and the natural beauty surrounding you come together to compose a visual symphony that transcends the ordinary.

Initiate the collaboration by articulating your vision for the elopement. Share your connection to nature, the specific landscapes that resonate with you, and the emotions you hope to convey through the imagery. The more transparent you are about your aspirations, the better equipped the photographer will be to align their creative approach with your unique vision.

Engage in a dialogue about the significance of the chosen outdoor setting. Whether it's a mountain vista, a windswept beach, or a secluded forest glade, each location holds its own magic. Communicate the personal meaning these landscapes hold for you as a couple—perhaps it's where you shared your first adventure or a place that symbolizes the serenity of your love. This exchange enriches the photographer's understanding, allowing them to infuse the images with a deeper sense of connection.

Discuss the story you want the images to tell. Nature is not just a backdrop; it's a character in the narrative of your elopement. Collaborate with the photographer to identify key moments that you wish to capture against the canvas of the natural setting. Whether it's the exchange of vows with a panoramic view in the background, the tender embrace under the shade of ancient trees, or the laughter echoing across a tranquil lake, these moments become the visual chapters that tell the story of your celebration.

Embrace spontaneity and allow room for the unexpected. While planning is crucial, nature has its own script, and sometimes the most magical moments are the unplanned ones. Collaborate with the photographer to remain open to spontaneous opportunities—whether it's an impromptu dance in a sunlit meadow, a playful interaction with wildlife, or a stolen kiss under a sudden burst of rain. These unscripted moments become the jewels in the crown of your elopement story.

Consider the role of natural elements in the imagery. Collaborate on how to incorporate the ever-changing elements of nature into the visual narrative. Whether it's capturing the play of light during different times of the day, using reflections in water to add depth, or embracing the drama of a passing storm, the collaboration between you and the photographer becomes a dance with the elements. Discuss your preferences for specific natural features—be it a cascade of fall foliage, a snow-kissed landscape, or the vibrant colors of spring blossoms.

Discuss the photographer's creative approach to working with nature. Each photographer has a unique perspective on how to harness the beauty of natural surroundings. Collaborate on their strategies for framing shots that showcase the grandeur of the landscape while preserving the intimacy of your connection. Whether it's using wide-angle lenses to capture sweeping vistas or opting for close-ups that highlight the details of the natural environment, this collaboration ensures a cohesive and visually compelling narrative.

Consider the timing of the elopement to align with natural phenomena. Collaborating on the timing of your elopement allows you to leverage the unique qualities of different seasons or natural events. Whether it's the vibrant colors of fall foliage, the ethereal glow of a summer sunset, or the crisp beauty of a winter landscape, the collaboration with your photographer involves strategic planning to synchronize your celebration with the rhythms of nature.

Discuss the logistics of navigating outdoor spaces. Collaborate on the practical aspects of moving through natural settings. Whether it's a gentle hike to a scenic spot, a stroll along the shore, or meandering through a wooded trail, discussing these logistics ensures that both you and the photographer are prepared for the physical aspects of capturing moments in outdoor environments. Collaboration in this regard enhances the overall experience and allows for a seamless flow between locations.

Lastly, trust the collaborative process. Your photographer is not just a documentarian; they are a creative partner invested in crafting a visual narrative that mirrors the authenticity and beauty of your love story within the embrace of nature. By approaching the collaboration with an open heart and a shared commitment to storytelling, you and your photographer will weave a tapestry of images that immortalize the essence of your elopement against the breathtaking backdrop of the great outdoors.

Capturing Candid Moments

In the enchanting realm of elopements, capturing candid moments is akin to preserving the spontaneous poetry of your love story—a delicate dance where every unscripted laugh, stolen glance, and heartfelt embrace is immortalized in the visual tapestry of your celebration. In this section, we explore the artistry behind capturing candid moments, weaving the raw and authentic threads of your connection into the fabric of your elopement imagery.

Candid moments are the heartbeat of visual storytelling—they are the unfiltered, genuine expressions that reflect the essence of your relationship. Collaborate with your photographer to create an atmosphere that encourages these organic moments to unfold naturally. Whether it's a quiet exchange of vows, a playful dance in a sunlit clearing, or a stolen kiss under the canopy of trees, these unscripted moments become the emotional anchors that define your elopement narrative.

Embrace the magic of spontaneity. Candid moments often arise when least expected—whether it's a shared chuckle over a lighthearted comment, an unguarded expression during an intimate conversation, or a stolen glance that speaks volumes. Encourage your photographer to be attuned to these spontaneous opportunities, allowing them to capture the unfiltered beauty of your connection without intrusion.

Create an environment of comfort and authenticity. The key to capturing candid moments lies in fostering an atmosphere where you and your partner feel at ease being your true selves. Whether it's the laughter that bubbles up naturally or the quiet moments of reflection, a comfortable environment allows for genuine expressions to shine through. Communicate with your photographer about your preferred level of involvement and any particular moments you wish to prioritize.

Consider the storytelling potential of every phase of your elopement day. Candid moments are not exclusive to the ceremony; they are woven throughout the entirety of your celebration. From the anticipation of getting ready to the adventurous escapades that follow the ceremony, each phase offers opportunities for unscripted moments. Collaborate with your photographer to outline the narrative arc of your elopement, ensuring that candid moments are seamlessly integrated into the visual storytelling journey.

Explore diverse locations for candid moments. While the ceremony site is undoubtedly significant, candid moments can unfold in various settings. Whether it's the intimacy of a secluded nook, the majesty of a panoramic viewpoint, or the simplicity of a forest path, diverse locations contribute to the richness of your elopement story. Collaborate with your photographer to identify key locations where candid moments can organically occur.

Incorporate movement into the storytelling. Candid moments often thrive in the interplay of movement and emotion. Whether it's a gentle walk hand in hand, a twirl under the open sky, or an adventurous exploration of the surroundings, movement adds a dynamic layer to candid captures. Collaborate with your photographer on how to incorporate movement into the visual narrative, allowing for a vibrant and expressive portrayal of your celebration.

Encourage authentic interactions with the environment. Nature provides a captivating backdrop for candid moments. Collaborate with your photographer to explore how you and your partner can authentically interact with the natural surroundings. Whether it's the joy of feeling the sand between your toes, the thrill of dancing in a field of wildflowers, or the serenity of a lakeside moment, allowing the environment to be an active participant enhances the authenticity of candid captures.

Trust the photographer's expertise in capturing the fleeting. Candid moments are, by nature, transient and ephemeral. Trust in your photographer's ability to navigate the ebb and flow of these moments, capturing the essence of your connection in the midst of the fleeting. Their skill in anticipating and reacting to these unscripted gems ensures that the visual narrative of your elopement is a genuine reflection of your love story.

Communicate openly about your preferences for candid photography. Each couple has a unique comfort level with candid captures. Some may prefer a more observational approach, allowing moments to unfold without interference, while others may welcome gentle guidance from the photographer. Collaborate with your photographer to articulate your preferences, ensuring that the approach aligns with your vision for candid moments during the elopement.

In the realm of elopements, capturing candid moments is an art form—an artistry that requires a collaborative dance between you, your partner, and your photographer. As you embark on this visual journey, open your hearts to the unscripted beauty of your connection, trusting that the candid moments captured will become the timeless chapters in the visual story of your extraordinary love celebration.

Encouraging natural and candid photography

Encouraging natural and candid photography is a collaborative endeavor that transforms your elopement imagery into a genuine and heartfelt visual narrative. In this exploration, we delve into the art of creating an atmosphere where unscripted moments unfold organically, capturing the true essence of your love story amidst the beauty of nature.

The foundation of natural and candid photography lies in fostering an environment of authenticity. As a couple, you are the heart of this narrative, and your connection serves as the guiding force. Communicate openly with your photographer about the importance of genuine moments and your desire for images that reflect the true spirit of your relationship. This transparent dialogue sets the stage for a collaborative journey where everyone is aligned in the pursuit of capturing authenticity.

Choose a photographer whose style resonates with your vision for natural and candid captures. Review their portfolio to ensure that their work showcases an adeptness in capturing unfiltered emotions and spontaneous moments. A photographer with a strong affinity for candid photography brings a unique skill set that goes beyond technical expertise—it involves an intuitive understanding of human connections and an ability to seamlessly blend into the background, allowing moments to unfold naturally.

Establish a rapport with your photographer before the elopement day. Building a connection with your photographer is akin to forging a friendship. Schedule engagement sessions or pre-elopement meetings to familiarize yourselves with their working style and to allow them to understand your dynamic as a couple. The more comfortable you are with your photographer, the more likely you are to exhibit natural expressions and behaviors during the elopement.

Communicate your story and vision for the day. Share the unique elements of your love story, the significance of the chosen outdoor setting, and any specific moments you envision capturing candidly. Providing this contextual understanding allows your photographer to approach the elopement with a deeper appreciation for the nuances of your connection and the narrative you wish to unfold.

Incorporate activities that evoke genuine emotions. Natural and candid moments often arise from activities that elicit authentic emotions. Plan elements of the day that resonate with your shared interests, whether it's a leisurely hike to a scenic spot, a picnic in a meadow, or a playful moment by the water. These activities become the canvas upon which your love story naturally unfolds, providing ample opportunities for candid captures.

Opt for an observational approach. Embrace the beauty of observation by allowing moments to transpire without interference. Encourage your photographer to adopt an observational stance, capturing the organic interactions and expressions that unfold naturally. This approach creates a visual narrative that feels unintrusive, allowing the true essence of your connection to shine through.

Minimize posed moments for a more genuine feel. While some posed shots may be essential, minimizing them allows for a more organic and genuine feel to the photography. Encourage your photographer to prioritize candid captures over posed setups, giving them the freedom to document the raw emotions and unscripted beauty of your elopement day.

Be present in the moment and forget about the camera. To capture the most authentic expressions, immerse yourselves fully in the present moment and forget about the presence of the camera. Engage with each other, connect emotionally, and savor the experience of your elopement day. When you're genuinely present, the camera becomes an unobtrusive witness to the natural and candid moments that unfold.

Embrace imperfections and unpredictability. Candid moments are inherently imperfect and unpredictable, and therein lies their charm. Embrace the imperfections, whether it's a tousled hair in the wind, a spontaneous burst of laughter, or a candid moment caught amidst unexpected weather. These elements contribute to the authenticity of the imagery, making it a true reflection of your elopement journey.

Celebrate the magic of the in-between moments. In-between moments are the heartbeat of natural and candid photography—the seconds between poses, the glances exchanged without words, and the subtle gestures that convey profound emotions. Encourage your photographer to celebrate these in-between moments, recognizing that they often hold the most genuine expressions and intimate connections.

In conclusion, encouraging natural and candid photography is about creating an environment where your love story can unfold authentically. Through collaboration, open communication, and a shared appreciation for the spontaneous beauty of the moment, you and your photographer will embark on a journey to capture the unfiltered, genuine, and timeless moments that define your extraordinary elopement celebration.

Creating a visual narrative of the outdoor elopement experience

Creating a visual narrative of the outdoor elopement experience is a captivating endeavor that transforms moments into a timeless story, capturing the essence of your celebration amidst the breathtaking backdrop of nature. In this exploration, we delve into the artistry of crafting a visual narrative that goes beyond individual images, weaving a tapestry that reflects the beauty, emotion, and unique journey of your elopement.

The visual narrative begins with the unfolding of your elopement day. Collaborate with your photographer to outline the narrative arc, identifying key moments and locations that hold significance for your love story. Consider the chronological flow of the day—from the anticipation of getting ready to the ceremony, post-ceremony adventures, and intimate moments shared between you and your partner. By establishing this narrative framework, your photographer can seamlessly weave together a cohesive and emotive story.

Embrace the full spectrum of emotions. The beauty of an elopement lies in its intimacy and the raw, genuine emotions that surface throughout the day. Collaborate with your photographer to ensure that the visual narrative captures a diverse range of emotions—from the quiet moments of reflection to the bursts of laughter, the tears of joy, and the serene expressions of love. Embracing the full spectrum of emotions ensures that your visual story is rich, authentic, and deeply resonant.

Explore the natural surroundings as characters in the narrative. Nature is not merely a backdrop; it's an integral character in the visual narrative of your elopement. Collaborate with your photographer to incorporate the natural surroundings as active participants in the story. Whether it's the vast expanse of a mountain range, the gentle rustle of leaves in a forest, or the reflective surface of a tranquil lake, allowing nature to play a role enhances the narrative's depth and connection to the environment.

Consider the transitions between locations and activities. The visual narrative gains depth through the seamless transitions between different phases of the elopement day. Collaborate on how these transitions are captured, whether it's the journey from the preparation site to the ceremony location, the post-ceremony adventures, or the intimate moments shared during a leisurely walk. These transitions become pivotal moments that contribute to the fluidity and storytelling rhythm of the visual narrative.

Incorporate visual motifs that symbolize your journey. Visual motifs serve as recurring elements that symbolize the themes and essence of your elopement experience. Collaborate with your photographer to identify motifs that hold personal significance—whether it's a particular flower, a symbolic piece of jewelry, or a specific landscape feature. These motifs create visual anchors within the narrative, adding layers of meaning and continuity to the storytelling.

Celebrate the spontaneity and unpredictability of nature. Nature, with its ever-changing moods, adds an element of unpredictability to the visual narrative. Collaborate with your photographer to embrace the spontaneous beauty that arises from unexpected weather, natural phenomena, or serendipitous moments. Whether it's capturing the dance of raindrops, the glow of a sudden sunbeam, or the play of shadows, these elements contribute to the narrative's authenticity and connection to the environment.

Utilize a mix of perspectives and compositions. Diversifying perspectives and compositions enhances the visual storytelling experience. Collaborate with your photographer to explore a mix of wide-angle shots that capture sweeping landscapes, close-ups that highlight intimate moments, and candid shots that convey genuine emotions. This variety creates a dynamic and visually engaging narrative that unfolds like a beautifully illustrated storybook.

Infuse the narrative with personal touches and details. The beauty of an elopement lies in its personalization. Collaborate on how to infuse the visual narrative with personal touches and details that reflect your unique journey. Whether it's incorporating sentimental items, cultural elements, or personalized vows, these details become integral chapters in the narrative, adding depth and authenticity to the visual story.

Consider the pacing and rhythm of the narrative. The pacing of the visual narrative influences the emotional impact and resonance. Collaborate with your photographer to consider the rhythm of the storytelling—whether it's the deliberate slowing down to savor intimate moments, the dynamic energy of adventure sequences, or the contemplative pauses that allow the emotions to linger. Pacing enhances the overall experience of the visual narrative, creating a cinematic flow that mirrors the ebb and flow of your elopement day.

Review and provide feedback on the storytelling process. Collaboration is an ongoing dialogue. As your photographer weaves together the visual narrative, engage in open communication, and provide feedback on the storytelling process. Share your thoughts on the sequencing of images, the emotional resonance of specific moments, and any additional elements you wish to incorporate. This collaborative exchange ensures that the final visual narrative is a true reflection of your vision and the unique essence of your outdoor elopement.

In conclusion, creating a visual narrative of the outdoor elopement experience is an artistic collaboration that goes beyond individual images. It is the crafting of a storytelling journey that immerses viewers in the beauty, emotion, and authenticity of your celebration amidst nature's grandeur. Through thoughtful collaboration, you and your photographer will embark on a visual storytelling adventure that becomes a cherished and timeless testament to the extraordinary moments of your elopement day.

Preserving Outdoor Memories

Preserving outdoor memories is an artful journey that extends beyond the elopement day itself. In this exploration, we delve into the significance of preserving the memories created amidst the natural beauty of your chosen outdoor setting—a journey that transforms moments into cherished keepsakes, ensuring that the essence of your elopement remains alive and vibrant for years to come.

Photography stands as the cornerstone of memory preservation. Collaborate with your chosen photographer to curate a collection of images that captures the magic, emotion, and breathtaking scenery of your outdoor elopement. Each photograph serves as a visual time capsule, transporting you back to the unique atmosphere and sentiments of your celebration. Emphasize the importance of candid shots, stunning landscapes, and intimate moments to create a comprehensive and evocative visual narrative.

Consider the tactile beauty of printed photographs. In the digital age, there's a certain enchantment in holding tangible memories. Explore the option of printing a selection of your favorite elopement photographs in various formats—whether it's a beautifully bound photo book, framed prints adorning your home, or a gallery wall that narrates the story of your outdoor celebration. Tangible prints add a tactile layer to your memories, inviting you to revisit and share the beauty of your elopement in a physical, touchable form.

Create a personalized wedding album or keepsake box. A custom wedding album serves as a curated showcase of the most significant moments from your elopement day. Collaborate with your photographer to design an album that tells the story of your celebration, combining images, captions, and perhaps even personal notes. Additionally, consider creating a keepsake box to house mementos from the day—whether it's dried flowers, a piece of the ceremony backdrop, or any other items that hold sentimental value.

Explore multimedia options to enhance storytelling. In addition to traditional photographs, explore multimedia options to enhance the storytelling experience. Consider incorporating video clips, audio recordings, or even a short film that captures the movement, sounds, and emotions of your outdoor elopement. These multimedia elements provide a dynamic and immersive way to relive the memories, allowing you to hear vows, laughter, and the ambient sounds of nature.

Commission artwork inspired by your outdoor celebration. Elevate the artistry of memory preservation by commissioning custom artwork inspired by your elopement. Engage with an artist to create a painting, illustration, or other visual representation that captures the unique atmosphere and emotions of your outdoor celebration. Artwork adds a personalized and artistic touch to memory preservation, transforming moments into timeless pieces of visual storytelling.

Document your elopement journey through a written narrative. Complement visual memories with the power of words by documenting your elopement journey through a written narrative. Craft a personal essay, letter, or journal entry that reflects on the emotions, experiences, and transformative moments of your outdoor celebration. Written words become a cherished companion to the visual memories, offering a nuanced and introspective perspective on your elopement.

Consider creating a dedicated digital archive. In the digital age, creating a dedicated digital archive ensures that your outdoor memories are easily accessible and shareable. Create a password-protected online gallery or a cloud-based archive where you can store high-resolution images, videos, and other digital memorabilia. This archive becomes a convenient and secure space to revisit your elopement memories, share them with loved ones, and ensure their preservation for years to come.

Celebrate anniversaries with meaningful reflections. Each anniversary becomes an opportunity to revisit and celebrate the memories of your outdoor elopement. Establish a tradition of meaningful reflections, whether it's revisiting your photo album together, watching your elopement video, or embarking on a return visit to the outdoor location where you exchanged vows. Anniversaries serve as poignant moments to reconnect with the emotions and beauty of your celebration.

Share your memories with loved ones. The joy of preserving memories amplifies when shared with loved ones. Invite friends and family to share in the magic of your elopement by organizing a post-celebration gathering, creating a digital slideshow, or even hosting a small viewing event. Sharing your memories creates a sense of community and allows others to witness the beauty of your outdoor celebration.

Reflect on the transformative power of outdoor memories. As time passes, reflect on the transformative power of your outdoor memories. Revisit your preserved photographs, albums, and keepsakes, allowing the memories to weave into the tapestry of your shared history. Acknowledge the impact that your elopement had on your relationship, growth as a couple, and the enduring connection to the natural world that became a backdrop to your love story.

In conclusion, preserving outdoor memories is an intentional and artful process that extends the life of your elopement celebration far beyond the day itself. Through a combination of visual storytelling, tangible keepsakes, multimedia elements, and personal reflections, you create a multidimensional archive that encapsulates the beauty, emotion, and significance of your outdoor journey. As you embark on this journey of preservation, you not only honor the memories of your elopement but also ensure that the magic of that extraordinary day remains a vibrant and cherished part of your shared history.

Creative ideas for preserving memories beyond photographs

Beyond the traditional realm of photographs, there lies a vast canvas of creative ideas for preserving the memories of your outdoor elopement—transforming moments into tangible, meaningful keepsakes that uniquely capture the essence of your celebration. In this exploration, we dive into inventive and heartfelt ways to immortalize your love story, allowing you to revisit the magic of your elopement through a myriad of creative avenues.

1. Customized Illustrations and Artwork: Commission a talented artist to create customized illustrations or artwork inspired by your elopement. Whether it's a watercolor rendering of your ceremony setting, an illustrated map of the outdoor location, or a stylized portrait capturing your unique love story, artwork adds a distinctive and artistic touch to memory preservation.

2. Pressed Flower Creations: Infuse a touch of nature into your memory preservation by incorporating pressed flowers from your elopement location. Create pressed flower arrangements, bookmarks, or even encapsulate delicate blooms in resin to fashion unique and timeless mementos that encapsulate the natural beauty of your outdoor celebration.

3. Audio Recordings of Vows and Moments: Capture the spoken words and ambient sounds of your elopement by recording audio snippets. Whether it's the exchange of vows, the rustle of leaves in the wind, or the laughter shared between you and your partner, audio recordings offer an immersive and emotional layer to memory preservation, allowing you to hear and relive the auditory essence of your celebration.

4. Personalized Keepsake Boxes: Design and create personalized keepsake boxes to house small mementos from your elopement day. Include items such as a piece of the ceremony backdrop, handwritten notes, or even symbolic trinkets. These curated keepsake boxes become cherished treasure chests that encapsulate the tangible elements of your outdoor celebration.

5. Handwritten Letters and Vows: Pen handwritten letters or vows to each other on your elopement day, expressing your emotions, dreams, and promises. Preserve these intimate writings in a beautifully bound journal or create a time capsule to be opened on future anniversaries. The power of handwritten words adds a personal and timeless dimension to memory preservation.

6. Customized Jewelry: Transform elements from your elopement location into customized jewelry. Consider incorporating stones, charms, or metals that hold significance to your outdoor setting. Whether it's a bracelet, necklace, or pair of earrings, these pieces become wearable tokens that carry the spirit of your elopement wherever you go.

7. Symbolic Planting or Tree Ceremony: Commemorate your elopement by planting a tree or a symbolic plant at the outdoor location where you exchanged vows. The act of planting becomes a living and growing representation of your love, and you can revisit the site over the years to witness the growth and vitality of the plant, mirroring the enduring nature of your relationship.

8. Handcrafted Ceremony Backdrop: If you had a handcrafted ceremony backdrop, consider repurposing it into a meaningful piece of decor for your home. Whether it becomes a wall hanging, a framed artwork, or even repurposed into a piece of furniture, the backdrop retains its significance while transforming into a functional and aesthetically pleasing reminder of your elopement.

9. Nature-Inspired Art Installations: Harness the natural elements of your elopement location to create art installations. Whether it's driftwood sculptures, pebble mosaics, or intricate sand designs, these nature-inspired installations serve as ephemeral yet captivating expressions of your love story within the context of the outdoor environment.

10. Adventure Scrapbooks: Go beyond traditional photo albums by creating adventure scrapbooks that chronicle the entire journey of your elopement. Incorporate not only photographs but also maps, pressed flowers, handwritten notes, and any other memorabilia that holds significance. Adventure scrapbooks become dynamic visual narratives, capturing the spirit of exploration and celebration.

11. Signature Scent Creations: Capture the essence of your outdoor elopement by creating signature scents or candles inspired by the natural aromas of the location. Whether it's the scent of pine, sea breeze, or wildflowers, these olfactory creations transport you back to the sensory experience of your celebration, adding a unique and evocative layer to memory preservation.

12. Outdoor Adventure Quilts: Transform the fabrics from your elopement attire or other meaningful textiles into a quilt or throw blanket. Each piece of fabric becomes a patch in the quilt, weaving together the threads of your outdoor adventure into a cozy and comforting keepsake that can be enjoyed for years to come.

In conclusion, creative ideas for preserving memories beyond photographs open up a world of possibilities, allowing you to encapsulate the unique beauty and emotions of your outdoor elopement in diverse and personalized ways. Whether through artistic endeavors, tangible mementos, or sensory experiences, these creative avenues enrich the tapestry of memory preservation, ensuring that the magic of your elopement remains alive and cherished through a multitude of expressive and meaningful forms.

Incorporating natural elements into keepsakes

Incorporating natural elements into keepsakes is a poetic and resonant way to infuse your elopement memories with the very essence of the outdoor setting where your love story unfolded. Nature, with its ever-changing beauty, becomes an integral part of the tangible treasures that symbolize the unique connection you share with each other and the natural world. In this exploration, we delve into the artistry of integrating natural elements into keepsakes, creating enduring reminders of the organic beauty that surrounded your outdoor celebration.

Pressed Florals as Timeless Reminders: Pressing flowers from your elopement location transforms delicate blooms into timeless keepsakes. Whether it's the vibrant petals of wildflowers, the ferns that adorned your ceremony site, or a small blossom from a significant tree, pressed florals encapsulate the ephemeral beauty of nature. Incorporate these pressed flowers into framed artwork, resin-encased pieces, or even within the pages of a cherished book—a tangible reminder of the flora that adorned your love-filled day.

Stones and Pebbles with Symbolic Significance: Gather stones or pebbles from the outdoor location where you exchanged vows, each carrying its own unique texture and energy. These stones can be transformed into personalized keepsakes, such as engraved markers, paperweights, or incorporated into jewelry. Each stone becomes a tangible link to the natural environment, anchoring your memories in the solid and enduring elements of the earth.

Wooden Keepsakes Crafted from Ceremony Elements: If your elopement involved handcrafted elements such as wooden ceremony backdrops or signage, consider repurposing these materials into lasting keepsakes. The weathered wood, adorned with memories of your celebration, can be transformed into wall art, decorative items, or even repurposed into functional pieces of furniture. The longevity of wood mirrors the enduring nature of your love story.

Custom Fragrances Inspired by the Outdoors: Capture the scent of the outdoors through custom fragrances that evoke the olfactory memories of your elopement location. Work with perfumers to create scents inspired by the natural aromas of the surroundings—whether it's the scent of pine, the freshness of the sea breeze, or the subtle notes of wildflowers. These custom fragrances become aromatic keepsakes, allowing you to immerse yourself in the sensory experience of your outdoor celebration.

Sand or Soil Encased in Resin: Collect a small amount of sand or soil from your elopement location and encase it in resin to create a visually striking and tactile keepsake. This encapsulation not only preserves the texture and colors of the earth but also serves as a tangible connection to the specific outdoor setting where you exchanged vows. The resin becomes a transparent window into the natural elements that ground your memories.

Dried Foliage as Botanical Tokens: Preserve the beauty of dried foliage, such as leaves or branches, from your elopement location. These botanical tokens can be incorporated into a variety of keepsakes, including shadow boxes, bookmarks, or even framed artwork. The dried foliage becomes a visual representation of the natural surroundings, frozen in time and encapsulated as a cherished memento.

Ceramic Pieces Molded from Outdoor Textures: Craft ceramic pieces, such as bowls, vases, or decorative items, molded with textures inspired by the outdoors. Capture the imprints of leaves, bark, or other natural elements in the clay to create unique and functional keepsakes. Each piece becomes a tangible expression of the organic textures that defined your outdoor celebration.

Handcrafted Paper Embedded with Natural Fibers: Commission handmade paper embedded with natural fibers from your elopement location. This artisanal paper can be transformed into personalized stationery, journals, or framed artwork. The integration of natural fibers adds an organic and textured layer to these keepsakes, becoming a tactile reminder of the raw beauty that surrounded your celebration.

Eco-Friendly Plantable Keepsakes: Opt for eco-friendly keepsakes that can be planted to grow into living reminders of your elopement. Seed-embedded paper, for instance, can be transformed into invitations, cards, or even small booklets. Once used, these plantable keepsakes can be planted to sprout wildflowers or herbs, creating a living testament to the natural elements that graced your celebration.

Natural Elements in Jewelry: Infuse natural elements directly into jewelry as a wearable expression of your elopement memories. Incorporate small stones, bits of wood, or even tiny vials of sand or soil into necklaces, bracelets, or rings. These pieces become intimate and portable tokens, allowing you to carry a piece of the outdoor setting with you wherever you go.

In conclusion, incorporating natural elements into keepsakes is a poetic and heartfelt way to weave the essence of the outdoors into tangible reminders of your elopement. Whether through pressed florals, stones with symbolic significance, fragrances inspired by the outdoors, or eco-friendly plantable creations, these keepsakes become more than mere objects—they are living connections to the natural world that witnessed the celebration of your love. As you embrace these nature-infused treasures, you not only preserve the memories of your elopement but also carry a piece of the outdoor magic with you throughout your journey together.

Chapter 6: Attire and Style

Chapter 6: Attire and Style

In the canvas of your elopement day, the attire you choose and the style you embrace become brushstrokes that paint a vivid and personal masterpiece. Chapter 6 delves into the world of "Attire and Style," where the threads of fashion intertwine with the natural beauty of your chosen outdoor setting. Like a tapestry woven with intention, your attire becomes a reflection of your unique love story and a harmonious dance with the elements that surround you.

As you step into this chapter, imagine your elopement attire not just as garments, but as a visual poem expressing the essence of your connection and the spirit of your outdoor celebration. From the rustle of the wind through the fabric to the play of sunlight on your chosen ensemble, every detail contributes to the visual symphony of your elopement day.

We'll explore how to seamlessly blend style with practicality, ensuring that your attire not only looks breathtaking but also enhances your comfort and mobility. Whether you're envisioning a flowing gown that mirrors the movement of the leaves or a suit that resonates with the rugged elegance of your outdoor locale, this chapter guides you in curating a look that feels both authentic and enchanting.

As we journey through the intricate details of attire and style, consider the cultural nuances and personal touches that can be woven into the fabric of your ensemble. Attire becomes a language of its own, narrating a story that transcends words and resonates with the surroundings. From the gentle sway of a bohemian-inspired dress to the crisp lines of a tailored suit against a mountain backdrop, each choice amplifies the visual poetry of your elopement.

Join us in Chapter 6 as we explore the artistry of attire and style, where the dress you wear and the details you choose become integral elements in the choreography of your elopement. Let the beauty of your attire harmonize with the natural setting, creating a visual composition that not only reflects your personalities but also celebrates the union of love and nature in every stitch and fold. As you embark on this exploration of style, envision yourself not just as a participant but as a living work of art, with your attire becoming a brushstroke that adds to the masterpiece of your elopement day.

Choosing Appropriate Attire

Choosing the appropriate attire for your elopement is akin to selecting the perfect ensemble for a dance—it should not only reflect your individual styles and preferences but should also harmonize effortlessly with the rhythm of your chosen outdoor setting. In this exploration of Chapter 6, we delve into the art of choosing attire that not only makes you feel confident and beautiful but also aligns seamlessly with the natural environment that will witness your celebration.

Consider the practicalities of your chosen outdoor location as you navigate the world of attire. If you're exchanging vows on a sandy beach, for instance, a flowing and lightweight dress may not only capture the ocean breeze beautifully but also allow for easy movement on the soft terrain. Alternatively, if your elopement unfolds amidst the grandeur of a mountain landscape, you might opt for attire that blends elegance with warmth, ensuring you stay comfortable in potentially cooler temperatures.

The fabric you choose becomes an integral aspect of the attire narrative. Flowing chiffons and lightweight lace, for instance, have an ethereal quality that complements outdoor settings. Fabrics that mimic the textures of nature, such as linen or organic cotton, not only offer visual appeal but also contribute to a tactile connection with the environment. Embrace the natural elements as your allies, allowing the wind to play with your gown or the sunlight to cast a gentle glow on your chosen fabrics.

Consider the color palette of your attire in conversation with the outdoor backdrop. While traditional whites and ivories are timeless and versatile, don't shy away from exploring subtle hues that resonate with the natural surroundings. Soft pastels, earthy tones, or even vibrant bursts of color can add a personalized touch to your ensemble while creating a harmonious visual composition with the outdoor landscape.

For the adventurous bride, explore attire options that embrace both style and practicality. Convertible dresses, with removable skirts or detachable trains, offer versatility for exploring different areas of your outdoor location. Jumpsuits or tailored separates can be both chic and functional, allowing for ease of movement during outdoor activities. Footwear, too, becomes a crucial element—consider comfortable yet stylish options that cater to the unique demands of your chosen terrain.

For the groom, the choice of attire can echo the rugged charm of the outdoors. Lightweight and breathable fabrics ensure comfort, while tailored suits or casual separates can strike the right balance between sophistication and a laid-back outdoor vibe. Don't be afraid to experiment with textures and patterns that add depth to the overall aesthetic.

As you navigate the vast landscape of attire options, remember that the key lies in authenticity. Your attire should feel like a natural extension of your personalities and the love story you share. Whether you envision a bohemian-inspired gown that mirrors the movement of leaves or a tailored suit that resonates with the rugged elegance of your outdoor locale, let your choices amplify the visual poetry of your elopement.

In conclusion, choosing appropriate attire for your elopement is a nuanced dance between personal style and the natural canvas that surrounds you. Let the fabric, color, and style of your ensemble become an expressive element in the visual symphony of your celebration, adding layers of meaning to each step you take in the outdoor landscape. As you embark on this sartorial journey, envision your attire not just as clothing but as a vessel for storytelling, where every stitch and fold contributes to the timeless tale of your love in the great outdoors.

Tips for selecting attire suitable for outdoor settings

Choosing attire for your outdoor elopement involves more than just picking beautiful garments—it's about ensuring that what you wear seamlessly integrates with the natural setting, allowing you to move freely and feel connected to the environment. Here are some tips to guide you in selecting attire that not only enhances your visual appeal but also aligns effortlessly with the outdoor backdrop.

Consider the practicalities of the location. If your elopement is set on a beach, flowing dresses or lightweight fabrics can capture the coastal breeze and allow for easy movement on the sandy terrain. For forest or mountain settings, where temperatures might vary, think about layers or dress options that strike a balance between elegance and warmth. This consideration ensures that you remain comfortable and adaptable to the elements throughout your celebration.

Embrace fabrics that complement the surroundings. Fabrics with a natural flow, such as chiffon or lace, can beautifully mimic the gentle movement of leaves or the sway of tall grass. Choosing materials that reflect the textures of nature, like linen or organic cotton, not only adds a tactile element to your attire but also creates a harmonious connection with the outdoor environment. The choice of fabric becomes an expressive component in the overall visual narrative of your elopement.

Think about color in conversation with the landscape. While traditional whites and ivories are timeless choices, don't hesitate to explore a palette that resonates with the natural surroundings. Soft pastels, earthy tones, or even vibrant hues can infuse your attire with a personalized touch while harmonizing with the colors of the outdoors. Let the natural backdrop influence your color choices, creating a cohesive and visually pleasing composition.

For the adventurous bride, consider practical and stylish options. Convertible dresses offer versatility, allowing you to adapt your look as you explore different areas of your chosen outdoor location. Jumpsuits or tailored separates provide a modern and functional alternative, ensuring ease of movement during outdoor activities. Pay attention to footwear—comfortable yet chic options that cater to the unique demands of your terrain can complete the look.

Grooms, too, can embrace the rugged charm of the outdoors in their attire choices. Opt for lightweight and breathable fabrics to ensure comfort, especially if your celebration involves physical activities. Tailored suits or casual separates strike a balance between sophistication and a laid-back outdoor vibe. Experiment with textures and patterns to add depth and interest to your ensemble.

As you navigate the plethora of attire options, authenticity should guide your choices. Your attire should feel like a natural extension of your personalities and the love story you share. Whether you envision a bohemian-inspired gown that mirrors the movement of leaves or a tailored suit that resonates with the rugged elegance of your outdoor locale, let your choices amplify the visual poetry of your elopement.

In summary, selecting attire suitable for an outdoor elopement is a delicate dance between personal style and the natural canvas that surrounds you. Let the fabric, color, and style of your ensemble become expressive elements in the visual symphony of your celebration, adding layers of meaning to each step you take in the outdoor landscape. As you embark on this sartorial journey, envision your attire not merely as clothing but as a vessel for storytelling, where every stitch and fold contributes to the timeless tale of your love in the great outdoors.

Embracing casual and unconventional styles

In the realm of outdoor elopements, there's a delightful freedom to embrace casual and unconventional styles that go beyond traditional wedding attire. This chapter invites you to explore the charm of laid-back elegance and the joy of unconventional choices, allowing your attire to reflect the unique spirit of your love story against the backdrop of nature's grandeur.

Casual doesn't mean sacrificing style—it's an invitation to let your personality shine through in your choice of attire. For brides, this might mean opting for a flowing bohemian dress that allows for easy movement and captures the carefree spirit of the outdoors. Consider dresses with unique textures, such as crochet or lace, that add a touch of individuality. Alternatively, jumpsuits or separates offer a modern and relaxed vibe while providing comfort for exploring your outdoor setting.

Grooms can also embrace casual styles that resonate with the relaxed atmosphere of an outdoor celebration. From tailored khakis paired with a crisp shirt to linen suits in earthy tones, there's a spectrum of options that balance sophistication with ease. Ditching the tie or opting for unconventional accessories, like patterned bow ties or leather suspenders, adds a playful touch to the overall look.

Unconventional styles provide an opportunity to step outside the conventional wedding attire box and truly showcase your personality. Consider bold colors or patterns that resonate with your tastes and the environment. Vibrant floral prints, earthy tones, or even denim can become part of your unique ensemble, contributing to a look that feels entirely authentic to you as a couple.

Accessories play a pivotal role in embracing casual and unconventional styles. For brides, flower crowns or natural foliage can add a whimsical and organic touch to your look. Consider skipping the veil and opting for a statement hat or even a pair of stylish boots that reflect your adventurous spirit. Grooms can experiment with non-traditional accessories like funky socks, personalized cufflinks, or even unconventional boutonnieres crafted from elements found in your outdoor setting.

Footwear becomes an exciting canvas for expressing casual and unconventional styles. Brides can trade traditional heels for comfortable yet stylish options like sandals, flats, or even bohemian-inspired barefoot sandals for a beach elopement. Grooms might consider eschewing formal shoes in favor of well-worn boots or stylish sneakers, adding a dash of personality to their ensemble.

The key to successfully embracing casual and unconventional styles lies in authenticity. Let your attire reflect who you are as a couple and what makes your love story unique. Whether it's a vintage-inspired dress that tells a story of its own or a groom's suit adorned with personal touches, these choices become part of the visual narrative of your elopement.

In conclusion, casual and unconventional styles open up a world of possibilities for expressing your individuality in the context of your outdoor elopement. It's an opportunity to celebrate your love in a way that feels true to you, breaking free from traditional norms and allowing your attire to mirror the genuine and intimate nature of your celebration. As you explore these non-traditional paths, remember that the most beautiful attire is the one that makes you feel authentically and joyfully you on this significant day of your lives.

Footwear and Accessories

As you venture into the realm of outdoor elopement attire, don't overlook the crucial role that footwear and accessories play in shaping your overall look. This section explores the delightful world of "Footwear and Accessories," where every step and accent becomes a brushstroke in the masterpiece of your elopement attire.

Let's start with footwear—an element often underestimated but with the potential to make a significant impact. For the bride, the choices are wonderfully diverse. If your celebration involves traversing sandy shores or meandering through grassy fields, consider eschewing traditional heels for more practical and comfortable options. Sandals, flats, or even barefoot styles adorned with delicate anklets can add a touch of bohemian charm while ensuring you move with ease and grace.

For the more adventurous bride, stepping into the wild might call for unconventional choices. Imagine exchanging vows in stylish boots that mirror the rugged landscape or embracing a beach elopement with barefoot sandals adorned with delicate shells. Your footwear becomes not just a practical consideration but an integral part of the narrative, allowing you to traverse your chosen outdoor setting effortlessly.

Grooms, too, have the opportunity to infuse personality into their ensemble through footwear. While classic formal shoes are a timeless choice, consider the terrain and setting. Well-worn boots can complement a rustic or mountainous backdrop, offering a rugged charm that aligns with the outdoors. Casual sneakers or loafers can be a stylish and comfortable choice for more laid-back settings, allowing you to move with comfort and confidence.

Accessories, like footwear, are the finishing touches that elevate your elopement look. For brides, flower crowns have become a popular choice, adding a touch of whimsy and nature-inspired elegance. Consider accessories crafted from natural elements found in your chosen environment—delicate ferns, wildflowers, or even feathers can be incorporated into headpieces or jewelry, creating a seamless connection with the outdoors.

Grooms can experiment with accessories that align with the casual and adventurous vibe of an outdoor celebration. Funky socks in bold patterns, personalized cufflinks, or unconventional boutonnieres crafted from local flora can inject personality into the groom's ensemble. Consider accessories that resonate with your interests and the unique story of your relationship, adding layers of meaning to your overall look.

In the dance between footwear and accessories, balance is key. Consider the overall aesthetic you want to achieve and how these elements contribute to the visual narrative of your elopement. Whether it's a barefoot bride adorned with a flower crown or a groom with rugged boots and a personalized boutonniere, every choice should feel authentic and in harmony with the natural surroundings.

As you navigate the realm of footwear and accessories, let your choices reflect not only your personal style but also the adventurous spirit of your love story. The little details—whether it's the crunch of gravel beneath your boots or the delicate rustle of leaves as you move—become part of the sensory tapestry of your elopement. Embrace the opportunity to step into this chapter with intention, letting each accessory and pair of shoes carry the weight of meaning as you embark on this beautiful journey of love and nature.

Practical considerations for outdoor footwear

When it comes to choosing outdoor footwear for your elopement, practicality takes center stage alongside style. As you embark on this adventure, let's delve into the considerations that will guide your selection, ensuring that every step you take is not only stylish but also well-suited to the natural terrain that frames your celebration.

For the bride, the first consideration is the nature of your chosen outdoor setting. If your elopement unfolds on a sandy beach or amidst lush grassy fields, traditional heels may pose challenges. Instead, opt for footwear that complements the environment—sandals or flats that allow you to move with ease on softer surfaces. Consider the ease of removal, especially if you plan to go barefoot for certain parts of the celebration, such as a beach ceremony.

For more adventurous terrain, such as rocky landscapes or mountainous trails, practicality becomes paramount. Stylish yet sturdy boots with good traction can provide the support needed for uneven surfaces. Choose footwear that not only aligns with your personal style but also ensures your comfort and stability as you traverse the outdoor landscape. Comfortable shoes become not just a practical choice but a necessity, allowing you to fully immerse yourself in the experience without the hindrance of discomfort.

Grooms, too, should consider the practicalities of the chosen setting when selecting footwear. If your elopement involves navigating different terrains, from forest trails to open fields, versatile footwear is key. Well-worn boots, perhaps with a touch of rustic charm, can be an excellent choice for a more rugged or natural setting. Casual sneakers or loafers may be suitable for less challenging terrains, allowing for both style and ease of movement.

Another crucial consideration for both brides and grooms is the weather. If your elopement takes place in an area prone to rain or unpredictable weather, waterproof or water-resistant footwear can be a game-changer. Soggy shoes can quickly dampen the joy of an outdoor celebration, so opting for weather-appropriate footwear ensures that you remain comfortable and focused on the moment, regardless of the elements.

Footwear that facilitates movement is particularly important for elopements with adventurous itineraries. Whether you plan to hike to a scenic viewpoint, explore a forest trail, or even dance under the open sky, your choice of shoes should enable you to engage fully in the experience. Consider how your footwear aligns with the activities you have planned, ensuring that each step is as effortless as it is stylish.

In summary, practical considerations for outdoor footwear revolve around the specific demands of your chosen elopement setting. Let the natural terrain guide your choices, ensuring that your footwear not only complements your overall look but also enhances your connection with the environment. Whether it's the soft embrace of sand beneath your feet or the sturdy support of boots against a rugged landscape, your shoes become an integral part of the narrative, allowing you to traverse the outdoors with confidence and grace. As you step into this chapter of your elopement journey, let practicality and style coalesce, creating a footwear ensemble that's as unforgettable as the love story it accompanies.

Stylish accessories that complement natural surroundings

Accessorizing for your outdoor elopement offers an exciting opportunity to blend style seamlessly with the natural surroundings. In this exploration of "Stylish Accessories That Complement Natural Surroundings," we navigate the nuances of choosing adornments that not only enhance your overall look but also harmonize with the breathtaking backdrop of your celebration.

For the bride, flower crowns have emerged as a beloved accessory that beautifully encapsulates the essence of outdoor weddings. These whimsical creations, adorned with delicate blooms and foliage, add a touch of ethereal beauty to your ensemble. Consider selecting flowers that mirror the local flora, creating a connection between your headpiece and the natural surroundings. A flower crown not only complements the environment but also infuses your look with a romantic and bohemian charm.

Incorporating natural elements into your jewelry can further elevate your connection to the outdoor setting. Delicate fern-inspired earrings, a pendant crafted from a tiny acorn, or a bracelet adorned with small stones can become symbolic tokens, seamlessly integrating with the landscape. Choose pieces that reflect the textures and colors of the surroundings, creating a cohesive and visually pleasing ensemble.

For the groom, accessories offer an opportunity to inject personality into the overall look while maintaining a connection to the outdoor theme. Consider unconventional boutonnieres crafted from local flora or elements found in the chosen setting. These distinctive boutonnieres not only add a unique touch but also serve as a nod to the environment, creating a visual link between your attire and the natural surroundings.

Funky socks can be another playful accessory for grooms, offering a pop of personality that complements the casual and adventurous vibe of outdoor elopements. Opt for bold patterns or colors that resonate with your personal style, adding a touch of fun to your ensemble. These small details contribute to a look that feels entirely authentic to you as a couple.

Both brides and grooms can explore the charm of incorporating natural elements into their accessories. Leather accessories, such as a wristband or cuff for the groom or a delicate leather wrap bracelet for the bride, can add a rustic and earthy touch. Consider engraving meaningful words or coordinates onto these pieces, creating keepsakes that tell a story of your elopement in the great outdoors.

Headpieces and hats provide an additional avenue for stylish adornment that complements the natural surroundings. Brides might opt for a statement hat that adds a touch of drama and offers practical sun protection, especially for elopements in open and sunny landscapes. Grooms can explore hats that align with the overall aesthetic, whether it's a classic fedora or a more casual wide-brimmed style.

As you select accessories for your outdoor elopement, consider the overall aesthetic you wish to achieve. Whether it's the gentle rustle of leaves in your flower crown, the earthy texture of a leather bracelet, or the vibrant hues of your floral-inspired jewelry, each accessory becomes a brushstroke in the canvas of your elopement look. Let your choices reflect not only your personal style but also the spirit of adventure that defines your love story against the backdrop of nature's grandeur.

Hair and Makeup for the Outdoors

In the enchanting realm of outdoor elopements, your hair and makeup choices become a delicate dance between expressing your individual style and aligning with the natural surroundings. This section, "Hair and Makeup for the Outdoors," unveils the artistry of creating a look that not only enhances your features but also resonates with the organic beauty of your chosen environment.

For the bride, the outdoor setting sets the stage for a more relaxed and natural approach to hair and makeup. Embrace the effortless elegance of loose waves or bohemian braids that seamlessly blend with the wind-kissed atmosphere. Consider opting for hairstyles that allow you to feel comfortable and unrestrained, especially if your elopement involves traversing uneven terrains or dancing under the open sky.

Natural makeup complements the outdoor setting by enhancing your features without overpowering them. Emphasize radiant and glowing skin, allowing your natural beauty to shine through. Soft and earthy tones for eyeshadow and lipstick can create a harmonious connection with the environment, evoking a sense of understated glamor that feels perfectly in tune with the outdoors.

Consider the season and climate of your chosen location when planning your hair and makeup. For warmer settings, embrace a sun-kissed glow with bronzed makeup tones and effortlessly tousled hair. In cooler climates, a more romantic and soft palette can enhance the cozy and intimate atmosphere of your elopement.

Grooms can also benefit from subtle grooming to ensure they look their best amid the natural backdrop. A light touch of makeup can help even out skin tones and reduce shine, ensuring a polished appearance in photographs. Grooming for the outdoors involves a careful balance—enhancing features without veering into overly dramatic territory.

Hair styling for grooms often leans toward the effortlessly groomed look, embracing natural textures and lengths. Consider a hairstyle that complements your overall aesthetic and aligns with the casual and adventurous vibe of an outdoor elopement. Grooming products can be used to maintain a polished appearance without sacrificing the relaxed atmosphere.

In the realm of outdoor elopements, the key is to strike a balance between polished and natural. Your hair and makeup choices should enhance your features while allowing you to move freely and authentically within the outdoor setting. Communicate openly with your hairstylist and makeup artist, sharing your vision and any considerations related to the climate or activities planned for the day.

It's advisable to schedule a trial session before the elopement to ensure that your chosen hair and makeup styles align seamlessly with your vision. Consider the longevity of your look, especially if your celebration extends from day to night. Waterproof or long-lasting products may be essential, especially if your elopement involves activities like hiking, beach strolls, or dancing under the stars.

As you step into the world of outdoor elopements, let your hair and makeup become an extension of your personality and the love story you're celebrating. Whether it's the gentle sway of loose curls in the breeze or the soft glow of natural makeup that captures the sunlight, your look should feel like an authentic reflection of the beautiful union between your love and the great outdoors.

Weather-proofing hair and makeup choices

Weather-proofing your hair and makeup choices is a thoughtful consideration that ensures you look and feel your best throughout the entirety of your outdoor elopement. As nature can be unpredictable, incorporating strategies to withstand different weather conditions becomes an integral part of crafting a resilient and beautiful look for your special day.

Let's start with the hair. If your elopement is set in an environment with potential wind or humidity, opt for hairstyles that are more resistant to these elements. Consider updos, braids, or structured styles that keep your hair secure and maintain their shape despite gusts of wind. Adding a touch of hairspray or a styling product can provide additional hold, keeping your hair in place and minimizing the impact of weather-related challenges.

For areas prone to rain or high humidity, incorporating anti-frizz products can be a game-changer. These products help control frizz and maintain a sleek and polished look, ensuring your hair remains picture-perfect even in less-than-ideal weather conditions. Communicate with your hairstylist about the climate of your chosen location, allowing them to select products and styles that align with the environmental factors you may encounter.

Makeup, too, can benefit from weather-proofing measures. If your elopement is set in a warmer climate or during the summer months, choosing long-wearing and sweat-resistant products is essential. Look for foundations, primers, and setting sprays that specifically cater to these conditions, providing a matte finish and preventing makeup from melting or shifting.

For elopements in cooler climates or during the fall and winter, hydrating and weather-resistant products can combat the effects of wind and cooler temperatures. A moisturizing primer, long-lasting foundation, and water-resistant mascara can be crucial elements in ensuring your makeup withstands the elements without compromising your desired look.

Waterproof makeup products are especially valuable for elopements near bodies of water or in locations prone to rain. Waterproof mascara, eyeliner, and even lip products can offer peace of mind, allowing you to embrace the moment without worrying about smudges or fading.

Planning for unexpected weather changes also involves having a touch-up kit on hand. Consider including blotting papers, a small mirror, and travel-sized versions of essential makeup products. This kit allows you to refresh your look throughout the day, ensuring you maintain the desired aesthetic even if the weather takes an unexpected turn.

Collaborating closely with your makeup artist is key to weather-proofing your look. Discuss the specific conditions of your chosen location and any potential challenges that may arise. Experienced artists can tailor their product selection and application techniques to enhance the longevity of your makeup in various weather scenarios.

Remember that embracing the elements can add a touch of authenticity and charm to your elopement photographs. Whether it's capturing the gentle flutter of loose curls in a breeze or raindrops glistening on your makeup, these natural elements become part of the unique story your images tell.

In the realm of weather-proofing your hair and makeup, the goal is not only to withstand the elements but also to ensure your look remains true to your vision throughout the entirety of your outdoor celebration. By taking these precautions and working collaboratively with your beauty team, you can confidently step into the unpredictable beauty of nature, ready to embrace every moment without compromising on style or resilience.

Achieving a natural and radiant look for outdoor ceremonies

Achieving a natural and radiant look for outdoor ceremonies involves a delicate balance between enhancing your features and allowing your authentic beauty to shine through. In the world of outdoor elopements, where nature provides a breathtaking backdrop, the goal is to create a makeup and hair look that seamlessly integrates with the surroundings while maintaining a fresh and radiant allure.

For a natural and radiant makeup look, start with a hydrating primer to create a smooth canvas for application. This ensures that your skin remains dewy and luminous, reflecting the natural light of the outdoors. Choose a foundation with a lightweight and buildable formula to achieve a radiant complexion without feeling heavy on the skin.

Emphasize radiant and glowing skin by incorporating subtle highlighter on the high points of your face. Opt for a highlighter with a soft and natural sheen, avoiding overly glittery or shimmery products for a look that feels effortless and in harmony with the outdoor setting. Soft, earthy tones for eyeshadow and a touch of mascara can enhance your eyes without overpowering your overall look.

Consider incorporating warm and neutral tones into your makeup palette to complement the natural surroundings. Soft browns, peaches, and muted pinks can add a touch of warmth to your look, creating a cohesive connection with the earthy elements of the outdoor environment. Blending these tones seamlessly allows your features to stand out while maintaining a natural and timeless elegance.

When it comes to achieving a natural and radiant look for your hair, embrace styles that enhance your natural texture and movement. Loose waves, tousled curls, or bohemian braids can effortlessly capture the relaxed and free-spirited vibe of outdoor elopements. Allow your hair to flow naturally, creating an ethereal and carefree feel that resonates with the beauty of nature.

Aim for a hairstyle that complements your chosen location. For beach elopements, consider beachy waves that mimic the natural texture of sea-kissed hair. In forest settings, opt for loose braids adorned with subtle florals that harmonize with the surrounding greenery. Your hairstylist can offer guidance on styles that suit your hair type and align with the overall aesthetic of your elopement.

To maintain a radiant look throughout the day, choose long-wearing and weather-resistant products. Setting sprays can help set your makeup, ensuring it stays in place even as you explore the outdoors. Additionally, consider incorporating hydrating and refreshing mists into your beauty routine, offering a quick pick-me-up to keep your skin glowing and rejuvenated.

Ultimately, the key to achieving a natural and radiant look for outdoor ceremonies lies in embracing your individuality and the unique setting of your elopement. Collaborate with your beauty team to share your vision and preferences, allowing them to tailor the makeup and hair choices to enhance your features while ensuring a look that feels perfectly at home in the great outdoors.

As you stand beneath the open sky or by the shoreline, let your makeup and hair radiate a timeless beauty that mirrors the authenticity of your love story. The goal is to feel effortlessly stunning, allowing your natural allure to shine through as you embark on this adventure of a lifetime against the backdrop of nature's grandeur.

Chapter 7: Personalizing Your Outdoor Ceremony

Welcome to Chapter 7, where the canvas of your outdoor elopement becomes a palette for personalization, allowing you to infuse your love story into every detail of the ceremony. "Personalizing Your Outdoor Ceremony" is a celebration of uniqueness and individuality, guiding you through the art of creating a ceremony that is a true reflection of your relationship and shared adventures.

In the vast expanse of nature, your love story takes center stage, and this chapter is your guide to painting the perfect picture. Whether you're exchanging vows beneath the rustling leaves of a forest canopy, on a windswept beach with the sound of waves as your soundtrack, or atop a mountain peak with the world at your feet, personalization is the brushstroke that transforms your elopement into an unforgettable masterpiece.

We understand that every love story is exceptional, and so should be your ceremony. This chapter unfolds a world of possibilities, from crafting meaningful vows that resonate with your journey to selecting readings that encapsulate the essence of your connection. Dive into the art of selecting music that harmonizes with the natural symphony around you, creating a soundtrack that becomes the melody of your love story.

Discover the magic of personalizing your ceremony decor, whether it's weaving in elements from your shared adventures, incorporating family heirlooms, or embracing DIY projects that add a touch of your personalities to the surroundings. Your outdoor ceremony is a canvas waiting to be adorned with details that make it uniquely yours.

Join us on this journey of personalization, where the beauty of your love story intertwines with the beauty of the great outdoors. Let the chapter ahead inspire you to infuse your outdoor ceremony with the essence of who you are as a couple, creating a moment that not only marks the beginning of your married life but also becomes a cherished memory etched against the backdrop of nature's grandeur.

Incorporating Nature into Decor

In the realm of personalizing your outdoor ceremony, there's a poetic dance that occurs when you seamlessly weave the beauty of nature into your decor. This isn't just about setting up an altar; it's about curating an immersive experience where the surroundings become an integral part of your love story. "Incorporating Nature into Decor" is the chapter that invites you to explore the enchanting possibilities of blending your celebration with the natural world that surrounds you.

Consider the venue as your canvas and nature as your artistic collaborator. Begin by embracing the existing elements of the outdoors. If you find yourself amidst towering trees, let the foliage become the backdrop for your ceremony. Allow the dappled sunlight to filter through the leaves, creating a natural and romantic ambiance. For beach settings, the sands can serve as your canvas, and the rhythmic waves provide an ever-changing backdrop that echoes the ebb and flow of your love.

Incorporating nature into your decor isn't just about adornments; it's about co-creating with the environment. Think about how the natural elements can play a role in defining the aesthetics of your ceremony. Consider floral arrangements that mimic the native blooms of the area, or driftwood accents that echo the coastal landscape. The goal is to enhance the existing beauty, not overshadow it.

For an ethereal touch, consider utilizing the natural surroundings for a ceremonial arch or canopy. Entwining branches, flowers, or fabric with the existing flora creates a seamless and organic extension of the environment. This not only adds a touch of whimsy but also serves as a visually striking focal point, framing your ceremony against the breathtaking backdrop of nature.

The beauty of this approach lies in its versatility. For forest elopements, you might choose to hang delicate fairy lights from the branches, creating a magical and intimate atmosphere as the day turns into night. By nightfall, let the gentle glow of lanterns guide your path, creating a romantic and otherworldly ambiance under the stars.

If your elopement embraces a mountainous terrain, consider utilizing the natural rocks or boulders as decorative elements. Adorn them with florals, greenery, or fabric that complements the color palette of the surrounding landscape. These subtle additions become harmonious accents, amplifying the grandeur of your mountainous backdrop.

In coastal settings, driftwood can become a versatile and charming decor element. Create arches or structures that mimic the natural curves of the shoreline, and adorn them with native florals or nautical-inspired accents. This not only blends seamlessly with the coastal environment but also allows you to embrace the character and charm of the beach.

In this chapter, nature isn't just a backdrop; it's an active participant in your ceremony. From the rustling leaves to the soothing sounds of the ocean, your decor becomes a dance with the elements. Embrace the simplicity and elegance that nature offers, allowing the outdoors to breathe life into every corner of your ceremony. The result is not just decor; it's an immersive experience where your love story unfolds in harmony with the natural world around you.

Creative decor ideas using natural elements

Infusing your outdoor ceremony with the charm of natural elements is an art that goes beyond conventional decor. It's about letting the authenticity of the surroundings inspire creative expressions that resonate with the core of your love story. In this section, we dive into the realm of "Creative Decor Ideas Using Natural Elements," exploring imaginative ways to bring the outdoors into your ceremony in unique and meaningful ways.

Start by considering the flora and fauna native to your chosen location. If you're nestled in a woodland paradise, explore the possibility of incorporating moss, ferns, or even fallen leaves into your decor. Adorn the ceremony aisle with arrangements of forest floor finds, creating a whimsical and enchanting pathway that immerses you and your guests in the beauty of the natural landscape.

For beach ceremonies, consider utilizing seashells, sand dollars, or pieces of driftwood as decor elements. Arrange them along the aisle, or use them to create captivating centerpieces. Seashell garlands can be a delightful addition to your ceremonial arch, adding a touch of coastal charm that harmonizes with the sounds of the waves in the background.

Embrace the versatility of rocks and stones in mountainous settings. Use them as placeholders, displaying your guests' names or well wishes. Create cairns or stone towers as symbolic representations of your journey, each rock a unique chapter in the story of your love. These natural elements not only add visual interest but also serve as grounding and symbolic components of your ceremony.

Let the color palette of your surroundings guide your decor choices. For desert elopements, consider incorporating sand-colored fabrics, succulents, and cacti. Use woven blankets or rugs to create a cozy and intimate space, mirroring the warm tones of the desert landscape. The juxtaposition of soft fabrics against the rugged backdrop of the desert adds a touch of luxury and comfort to the ceremony setting.

Incorporating wildflowers into your decor can add a burst of color and an air of untamed elegance. Select blooms that are local to the area and in season, allowing your decor to harmonize with the natural rhythm of the landscape. Arrange wildflowers in bouquets, scatter petals along the aisle, or even create floral crowns for an added touch of romance.

Consider utilizing fallen branches or twigs to create unique and rustic decor pieces. Twine them together to form arches or arbors, or repurpose them as natural aisle markers. Hang small glass jars filled with delicate flowers from the branches, allowing the gentle sway in the breeze to become part of the natural symphony of your ceremony.

For a celestial touch, consider incorporating celestial elements like feathers or crystals into your decor. Hang dreamcatchers adorned with feathers from tree branches for a bohemian and ethereal aesthetic. Crystals, whether incorporated into table centerpieces or scattered along the ceremony space, can add a touch of mystique and magic to the overall ambiance.

The key to creative decor using natural elements is to let your imagination run wild while staying attuned to the unique features of your chosen location. Allow the textures, colors, and shapes of the outdoors to guide your choices, creating a ceremony space that feels like an organic extension of the environment. This approach not only adds a personalized touch to your decor but also creates an immersive experience where the beauty of nature intertwines seamlessly with the celebration of your love.

Enhancing the outdoor setting without overshadowing its beauty

Enhancing the outdoor setting for your elopement is a delicate dance between adding personal touches and allowing the inherent beauty of nature to shine. In this section, "Enhancing the Outdoor Setting Without Overshadowing Its Beauty," we explore the art of harmonizing your decorative elements with the surroundings, ensuring that every detail contributes to the magic of the moment without detracting from the natural splendor.

Nature serves as a breathtaking backdrop for your ceremony, offering a canvas that's already adorned with the grandeur of mountains, the serenity of beaches, or the enchantment of forests. The challenge lies in enhancing this canvas without overwhelming it. Think of your decor as accents that highlight and complement, not compete with, the outdoor beauty.

Consider starting with minimalist decor that accentuates rather than dominates the landscape. This could involve simple arrangements of local flowers, strategically placed lanterns, or ethereal drapery that gently billows in the breeze. The goal is to let the natural setting take center stage while your decor works to enhance, not distract.

Lighting plays a pivotal role in accentuating outdoor spaces without overshadowing their inherent charm. For evening ceremonies, consider the subtle glow of string lights or lanterns that cast a warm and inviting ambiance. Illuminate pathways and focal points with soft lighting, allowing the natural elements to play with shadows and create an enchanting atmosphere.

When it comes to enhancing the ceremony area, opt for decor that integrates seamlessly with the surroundings. Consider a ceremonial arch made of natural materials like driftwood, adorned with a touch of florals that mimic the local blooms. This way, the structure becomes an extension of the landscape rather than an imposition on it.

In beach settings, where the sands themselves are a vital part of the allure, tread lightly with decor choices. Use natural materials like bamboo or woven elements for arches or aisle markers, allowing them to blend harmoniously with the coastal backdrop. Incorporate elements that echo the sea, such as delicate seashell accents or breezy fabric that mimics the movement of ocean waves.

For forest elopements, let the towering trees and lush greenery guide your decor choices. Consider incorporating elements like tree stumps or natural rocks as ceremonial markers. Embrace the earthy tones of the surroundings with soft fabrics and understated floral arrangements that add a touch of romance without detracting from the forest's innate beauty.

Maintaining a color palette that complements the natural landscape is essential. Earthy tones, muted hues, and pastels can seamlessly merge with the outdoors, creating an atmosphere that feels organic and cohesive. Think about the colors of the season and how your chosen decor can reflect and enhance the natural palette.

Another way to enhance the outdoor setting is to utilize the existing features of the location. If you're surrounded by water, consider floating decor elements or reflective surfaces that mirror the surroundings. Use the branches of trees or existing structures as anchor points for decor, minimizing the need for additional installations that could distract from the landscape.

Remember, the goal is not to transform the outdoor setting into an entirely different space but to elevate it in a way that feels organic and authentic. Your decor should complement the landscape, allowing the two to dance in harmony as you exchange vows amidst the beauty of nature. In doing so, you create a ceremony space that is not just visually stunning but emotionally resonant, where every element contributes to the immersive experience of celebrating love in the great outdoors.

Writing Personal Vows

In the tapestry of your outdoor elopement ceremony, the exchange of vows stands as the most intimate and personal thread. "Writing Personal Vows" is a chapter that delves into the art of crafting promises that go beyond the traditional, capturing the essence of your unique love story amidst the grandeur of nature.

Personal vows are an opportunity to express the depths of your emotions, the quirks of your relationship, and the shared dreams that have led you to this moment. Writing them for an outdoor ceremony adds an extra layer of significance, as your words become part of the natural symphony that surrounds you—whispered to the wind, echoed by the trees, and sealed with the backdrop of majestic landscapes.

Start by reflecting on the journey that brought you both to this enchanting outdoor setting. Consider the shared experiences that have shaped your love—the laughter, the challenges, the quiet moments of understanding. Use these reflections to form the foundation of your vows, creating a narrative that is uniquely yours.

For couples who are drawn to the mountains, infuse your vows with the strength and endurance that these majestic peaks symbolize. Speak of the unwavering support you promise, like the mountains that stand tall against the test of time. Express your commitment to exploring the peaks and valleys of life together, hand in hand.

If your elopement unfolds on the beach, let the rhythm of the waves inspire the cadence of your vows. Promise to be the constant in each other's lives, just as the ocean kisses the shore with unwavering devotion. Paint a picture with your words, imagining your love as vast and boundless as the sea.

For those surrounded by the embrace of a forest, draw inspiration from the evergreen trees that endure through all seasons. Speak of growth, renewal, and the promise to stand by one another as you navigate the twists and turns of life's journey. Let your vows be as timeless as the ageless trees that bear witness to your promises.

Consider incorporating elements from your outdoor surroundings into your vows. Mention the warmth of the sun, the gentle rustle of leaves, or the scent of wildflowers. These details anchor your promises in the present moment, creating a connection between your love and the nature that envelops you.

Embrace vulnerability in your vows. Share the qualities you adore in each other and the moments that have etched themselves into your hearts. Express gratitude for the support, joy, and comfort your partner brings to your life. Let your vulnerability be a testament to the authenticity of your love.

Crafting personal vows is not about perfection; it's about sincerity. Be true to your feelings, and don't shy away from humor, tenderness, or even a touch of poetic flair. Your vows are a celebration of your unique love story, and they should resonate with the authenticity that defines your relationship.

As you stand beneath the open sky or beside the lapping waves, let your words be a tribute to the beauty of the moment and the enduring commitment you make to each other. The magic of personal vows lies in their ability to transcend the ordinary, creating a connection that echoes through the vastness of nature and lingers in the hearts of those who bear witness to your love. In this chapter, discover the joy of pouring your heart into words, crafting promises that will become an integral part of the landscape where your love story unfolds.

Crafting heartfelt vows inspired by nature

Crafting heartfelt vows inspired by nature adds an extra layer of poetic beauty to the already profound act of expressing your love. In this section, we explore the art of "Crafting Heartfelt Vows Inspired by Nature," inviting you to infuse your promises with the essence of the outdoors, creating a symphony of emotions that resonates with the natural world surrounding your elopement.

Begin by immersing yourself in the sights, sounds, and sensations of the outdoor setting where you'll exchange vows. Close your eyes and feel the breeze on your skin, listen to the rustle of leaves or the gentle lapping of waves, and breathe in the scents carried by the air. Let these sensory experiences guide the tone and imagery of your vows.

Draw parallels between the elements of nature and the qualities of your relationship. For example, if your ceremony takes place in a blooming meadow, you might weave in metaphors of growth and blossoming, expressing how your love has flourished like wildflowers in the springtime. Speak of the vibrant colors and fragrances that mirror the richness of your shared experiences.

Consider the symbolism of natural elements as you craft your vows. The steadfastness of a mountain can inspire promises of unwavering support and resilience. You might say, "Just as the mountain stands tall against the changing seasons, I promise to be your constant, facing life's peaks and valleys by your side."

If surrounded by the soothing sounds of a flowing river, incorporate the fluidity of water into your vows. Promise to navigate the currents of life together, adapting and flowing with the inevitable changes. Let the rhythmic nature of a river guide the rhythm of your words, creating a cadence that echoes the eternal flow of your love.

Incorporate the cycles of nature into your vows, mirroring the cyclical nature of relationships. Speak of the changing seasons as metaphors for the various phases of your love—the warmth of summer, the introspection of autumn, the freshness of spring, and the resilience of winter. Promise to embrace each season with the same devotion.

Let the natural beauty around you inspire vivid and picturesque language. Describe your partner's eyes as deep as the ocean, their laughter as melodious as a songbird, or their touch as gentle as a breeze. Use descriptive imagery to paint a vivid portrait of your love, creating a sensory experience for both you and your partner.

Invoke the symbolism of the sun, moon, and stars into your vows. Promise to be each other's guiding light in moments of darkness, to be the constant star that leads one another home. This celestial imagery adds a touch of cosmic romance to your promises, connecting your love to the vastness of the universe.

Consider the flora and fauna present in your chosen outdoor setting. If surrounded by trees, speak of your love as strong and enduring, rooted deeply like the ancient oaks. If in a garden, liken your relationship to a delicate bloom, promising to nurture and cherish each other as the most precious of flowers.

As you craft these nature-inspired vows, let your heart guide your pen. Don't be afraid to be poetic, whimsical, or deeply sentimental. Your words are a celebration of the unique love story you share, and infusing them with the magic of nature adds an unforgettable dimension to your vows. Ultimately, your heartfelt promises become not only a declaration of love but also a poetic tribute to the beauty that surrounds you on this special day.

Incorporating personal stories into the ceremony

Incorporating personal stories into your ceremony is akin to weaving a tapestry of your shared history, creating a narrative that resonates with authenticity and depth. This section explores the art of "Incorporating Personal Stories into the Ceremony," offering you a guide on how to infuse your vows with the richness of your unique journey together.

Begin by reflecting on the moments that have defined your relationship—the laughter, the challenges, the unexpected adventures, and the quiet moments of understanding. These stories are the threads that have woven your love into a beautiful tapestry, and sharing them during your ceremony allows you to invite your loved ones into the heart of your connection.

Choose anecdotes that hold particular significance for both of you. Whether it's the first time you met, a transformative trip you took together, or a shared accomplishment, these stories become the building blocks of your vows. Select narratives that capture the essence of your relationship, showcasing the qualities and experiences that have strengthened your bond.

Consider the setting of your elopement and how it aligns with the stories you want to share. If you're surrounded by the towering peaks of a mountain range, narrate the tale of a challenging hike that became a metaphor for your journey through life's challenges. If your ceremony unfolds on a tranquil beach, recount a memorable seaside moment that symbolizes the serenity of your love.

Craft your storytelling with a balance of humor, sentimentality, and authenticity. Share the quirks that make your relationship uniquely yours—the inside jokes, the playful banter, and the endearing idiosyncrasies that have become cherished facets of your connection. Let your stories reflect the full spectrum of your emotions, from the lighthearted to the profound.

As you share these personal narratives, invite your guests to join you on a journey through the chapters of your love story. Paint vivid pictures with your words, transporting them to the moments that have shaped your relationship. Create a sense of intimacy, allowing those present to feel like honored witnesses to the unfolding of your narrative.

While personal stories inject warmth and familiarity into your vows, ensure that they remain inclusive for your guests. Provide enough context to make the anecdotes relatable, allowing friends and family to connect with the emotions and sentiments you express. This inclusivity enhances the collective experience, fostering a deeper connection between you, your partner, and your loved ones.

Consider alternating storytelling with more traditional vows or promises to maintain a balance in tone. The personal stories act as interludes, punctuating the ceremony with moments of laughter, reflection, and tenderness. This dynamic structure keeps the ceremony engaging and ensures that each element serves a purpose in conveying the depth of your commitment.

Ultimately, incorporating personal stories into your ceremony is an invitation to share the chapters of your love story with those who matter most. It transforms your elopement from a mere exchange of vows into a communal celebration of your unique connection. By intertwining personal narratives with promises for the future, you create a ceremony that is not only a declaration of love but also a testament to the rich tapestry of your shared history.

Symbolic Rituals in Nature

Engaging in symbolic rituals amidst the embrace of nature can infuse your ceremony with profound meaning, creating a tapestry of shared experiences and shared intentions. In this exploration of "Symbolic Rituals in Nature," we delve into the transformative power of incorporating meaningful actions into your elopement, deepening the significance of your commitment to one another.

Nature itself is a canvas for symbolism, offering myriad elements that can be woven into your ceremony. Begin by contemplating the elements that hold personal significance for both you and your partner. Whether it's the earth beneath your feet, the water flowing nearby, the warmth of the sun, or the whispers of the wind, each element carries its own symbolism that can be harnessed to enhance the ritual.

Consider a grounding ritual that involves collecting soil or stones from a location significant to your relationship. As you exchange these elements during the ceremony, you symbolize the merging of your individual lives into a shared foundation. This act serves as a tangible representation of your commitment to build upon the solid ground of your love.

Embrace the fluidity of water as a symbol of cleansing and renewal. This can take the form of a water-sharing ritual where you pour water from two separate vessels into a single container, signifying the merging of your individual lives into a harmonious union. The flowing water represents the continuous ebb and flow of your shared journey.

The warmth and energy of the sun can be incorporated into a ritual that involves passing a small flame between you and your partner. As the flame passes, you express the warmth and light that your love brings into each other's lives. This symbolic gesture represents the sharing of your inner fire and the promise to keep each other's hearts aglow.

Explore the symbolism of planting seeds or saplings together. As you nurture the growth of a new life, it becomes a metaphor for the flourishing of your relationship. This ritual aligns with the cycle of nature, as you witness the growth and transformation of the planted seeds mirroring the evolution of your shared life together.

For couples drawn to the air and the wind, consider a ritual involving the exchange of written vows. As the pages flutter in the wind, your words become ethereal, carried away like messages to the universe. This symbolic act emphasizes the ephemeral nature of life while etching your promises into the ever-changing canvas of the world.

Incorporate the surrounding flora into your symbolic rituals. Exchange flower garlands or create a unity bouquet by each adding a bloom, symbolizing the intertwining of your individual identities into a harmonious partnership. This gesture is not only visually stunning but also represents the blooming of your shared love.

Engage in rituals that involve the passage of time, such as an hourglass ceremony. As the sand flows from one chamber to another, you symbolize the eternal and ever-changing nature of your love. This visual representation becomes a poignant reminder of the journey you are embarking on together.

Whichever symbolic ritual you choose, ensure it aligns with the essence of your relationship and the natural surroundings of your elopement. These rituals transcend the ordinary, transforming your ceremony into a sacred space where the elements of nature become witnesses to your commitment. As you engage in these symbolic acts, you not only create lasting memories but also anchor your vows in the profound symbolism of the natural world, weaving an enduring tapestry of love and connection.

Exploring rituals that connect with the environment

Exploring rituals that intimately connect with the environment adds a unique layer of depth and resonance to your elopement ceremony. In this exploration of "Rituals Connecting with the Environment," we delve into ways to infuse your vows with the spirit of nature, forging a profound connection between your commitment and the surrounding world.

Consider a ritual that involves the exchange of natural elements. Embrace the earth beneath your feet by exchanging small containers of soil or stones. As you pour these elements into a shared vessel, you symbolize the blending of your individual essences into a solid foundation. This act resonates with the grounded nature of your commitment, emphasizing the strength and stability of your love.

Water, with its symbolic connotations of purity and renewal, can be incorporated into a ritual that connects with the environment. Picture a water-sharing ceremony where you each pour water from separate vessels into a common container. As the waters mingle, you signify the merging of your lives into a harmonious flow, much like the interconnected streams of nature.

If your ceremony unfolds in a location with a significant breeze, explore a ritual involving the exchange of written vows. As you read your promises, release the written words to the wind. Watch as the pages flutter away, carrying your heartfelt expressions into the air. This ritual not only celebrates the ephemeral nature of life but also marks your vows as messages carried to the universe.

Engage with the surrounding flora by incorporating flower garlands or creating a unity bouquet. Exchange these botanical tokens, symbolizing the intertwining of your individual identities into a harmonious partnership. This gesture not only embraces the beauty of nature but also signifies the blooming of your shared love, mirroring the growth and blossoming of the natural world.

For those drawn to the symbolism of time, consider a ritual involving an hourglass. As the sand flows from one chamber to another, you symbolize the eternal and ever-changing nature of your love. The visual representation of time becomes a poignant reminder of the journey you are embarking on together, anchored in the passage of moments.

Planting seeds or saplings together is another eco-conscious ritual. As you nurture the growth of new life, you metaphorically represent the flourishing of your relationship. This act aligns with the cyclical nature of nature, emphasizing the evolution and transformation of your shared life.

An exploration of rituals connecting with the environment encourages you to be mindful of the specific characteristics and surroundings of your elopement location. Tailoring your rituals to the natural elements present not only enhances the symbolism but also allows you to harmonize with the unique energy of the environment.

As you engage in these rituals, you not only celebrate your love but also become active participants in the larger narrative of nature. Your vows and promises become intertwined with the landscape, creating a tapestry of commitment woven into the very fabric of the natural world. In doing so, your elopement transcends a mere ceremony; it becomes a symbiotic exchange between your love and the environment, leaving an indelible mark on the canvas of your shared journey.

Creating lasting memories through symbolic gestures

Creating lasting memories through symbolic gestures infuses your elopement with depth and significance, turning it into a cherished tapestry of shared experiences. In this exploration of "Creating Lasting Memories through Symbolic Gestures," we delve into ways to etch the magic of your commitment into the annals of your relationship, crafting enduring memories that will resonate throughout your journey together.

One profound way to solidify memories is through a unity ceremony involving the creation of a time capsule. Choose meaningful items or handwritten notes that encapsulate the essence of your love and commitment. As you seal the capsule during the ceremony, you symbolize the preservation of this moment in time, to be revisited on future anniversaries. This ritual not only creates a tangible representation of your love but also becomes a treasure trove of memories waiting to be uncovered in the years to come.

Another touching gesture involves releasing biodegradable balloons or lanterns into the sky. Each balloon or lantern represents a shared wish, dream, or intention for your life together. As they ascend, carrying your collective hopes into the atmosphere, you create a visually poetic representation of your shared aspirations. This act not only becomes a beautiful spectacle but also leaves an indelible mark in the skies, symbolizing the boundless potential of your journey together.

Consider crafting a custom piece of art during the ceremony. Choose a medium that resonates with both of you—whether it's painting, sculpting, or crafting. As you collaboratively create this piece, you infuse it with the energy of the moment, turning it into a tangible expression of your union. The finished artwork becomes a visual reminder of the emotions and intentions shared during your elopement, hanging proudly in your shared space.

For couples drawn to the celestial wonders, stargazing can become a symbolic gesture of infinite love. If your elopement occurs under a starry sky, take a moment during the ceremony to gaze at the constellations above. Symbolically, you align your love with the timeless beauty of the cosmos, creating a celestial connection that transcends earthly boundaries. This act not only becomes a shared experience but also transforms the stars into witnesses of your eternal commitment.

Engaging in a collaborative art project, such as creating a handcrafted vow book, offers a tangible keepsake from your elopement. Decorate the book with mementos collected from the location, pressed flowers, or small tokens that represent your shared journey. As you exchange vows within its pages, you imbue the book with the emotional resonance of the moment, creating a cherished relic that will transport you back to your elopement day each time you revisit it.

These symbolic gestures are not only memorable but also contribute to the narrative of your relationship. By infusing your elopement with intentional actions and shared experiences, you not only create an unforgettable day but also lay the foundation for a legacy of love. As you embark on this journey together, may these gestures serve as touchstones, guiding you back to the profound commitment and magic that unfolded on the day you declared your love amidst the beauty of the outdoors.

Chapter 8: Family and Friends

In the heart of every elopement lies the essence of shared joy, and in Chapter 8, we explore the vital role that family and friends play in turning your outdoor celebration into a collective tapestry of love. Titled "Family and Friends," this chapter invites you to consider the various ways your loved ones can contribute to and enhance your intimate elopement experience.

Eloping doesn't mean excluding those closest to your heart; instead, it's an opportunity to forge meaningful connections in an intimate setting. This chapter delves into the art of blending the magic of nature with the warmth of human connection, ensuring that your chosen company becomes an integral part of the unforgettable narrative you're weaving on this special day.

From sharing the joy of your commitment amidst the grandeur of the outdoors to involving family and friends in the ceremony itself, we explore how their presence adds layers of love to your celebration. Whether it's creating cherished memories with select loved ones, engaging in meaningful rituals, or finding unique ways to include absent friends, this chapter is a guide to turning your elopement into a shared experience that resonates with the bonds of family and friendship.

As you navigate the intricate dance between the serenity of nature and the embrace of your loved ones, this chapter serves as a compass, helping you strike the perfect balance. Because, after all, an elopement is not just about the couple; it's a celebration that echoes with the collective laughter, support, and love of those who matter most. Let's embark on a journey that intertwines the beauty of the outdoors with the warmth of familial and friendly ties, creating a celebration that is as rich and diverse as the relationships that shape your world.

Communicating Your Choice to Elope

Embarking on the journey of elopement can be a deeply personal and profound choice. However, communicating this decision to family and friends requires a delicate touch and thoughtful consideration. In this exploration of "Communicating Your Choice to Elope," we delve into the nuances of sharing this intimate decision with your loved ones, ensuring that your elopement is met with understanding, support, and perhaps even shared excitement.

Initiating a conversation about your choice to elope involves transparency and a genuine expression of your feelings. Start by reflecting on the reasons behind your decision, whether it's the desire for an intimate celebration, the wish to connect with nature, or the pursuit of a unique and personal experience. Being clear about your motivations will help convey the authenticity of your choice, allowing your loved ones to better understand your perspective.

Choose an appropriate time and setting for the conversation, providing a relaxed and open environment for discussion. Whether it's a casual family gathering or a heartfelt one-on-one conversation, setting the stage for open communication is key. Express your emotions honestly, emphasizing the personal significance that an elopement holds for you and your partner.

Anticipate a range of reactions from your loved ones, acknowledging that responses may vary. Some might be initially surprised or even taken aback, while others may readily embrace the idea. Be patient and open to addressing any concerns or questions that arise. Offering reassurance about your commitment to maintaining the bonds with family and friends, despite choosing an intimate ceremony, can go a long way in fostering understanding.

Share the vision you have for your elopement day, highlighting the elements that make it special and meaningful to you. Whether it's the breathtaking scenery, the opportunity for a more profound connection with your partner, or the chance to celebrate your love in a way that aligns with your values, communicating the essence of your elopement helps others appreciate the depth of your decision.

Consider involving your loved ones in aspects of the elopement planning process. This could range from seeking their input on certain elements, such as location or date, to finding ways for them to contribute to the celebration. In doing so, you invite them to be a part of the journey, fostering a sense of inclusion and shared excitement.

Throughout the conversation, emphasize the enduring nature of your relationships. Assure your loved ones that while the ceremony may be intimate, your commitment to maintaining and nurturing your connections with them remains unwavering. By framing the elopement as an extension of your love story rather than a departure from familial bonds, you reinforce the idea that this choice is about crafting a celebration that authentically reflects your relationship.

In essence, communicating your choice to elope is an opportunity to share the profound meaning behind your decision with those who matter most. Approach the conversation with sincerity, a willingness to address concerns, and an invitation for loved ones to be part of the journey in ways that resonate with them. As you navigate these conversations, remember that each relationship is unique, and by expressing your truth with love and openness, you pave the way for understanding and shared joy.

Addressing potential concerns from family and friends

In the delicate process of communicating your choice to elope, it's important to anticipate and address potential concerns that family and friends might have. Understandably, this decision might evoke various emotions and questions, and by proactively acknowledging and addressing these concerns, you can foster a deeper understanding and support for your choice.

One common concern that may arise is the feeling of exclusion. Loved ones might worry that an intimate elopement means they won't be part of a significant milestone in your life. To address this, emphasize that while the ceremony itself may be more private, your commitment to your relationships remains unchanged. Reassure them that you value and cherish their role in your life, and that the decision to elope is about creating a celebration that aligns with your personal values and desires.

Financial considerations could also be a source of concern. Some family members may worry about the expenses associated with destination elopements or celebrations in unique outdoor settings. Openly discuss your budget and financial plan, and express that your choice to elope is not a reflection of wanting to exclude anyone due to financial constraints. Emphasize that the focus is on creating a meaningful and personal experience rather than an extravagant event.

Another concern may revolve around the idea of traditions and expectations. Loved ones might wonder why you're deviating from the more conventional path of a traditional wedding. Take the time to explain your desire for an authentic and unique celebration that reflects your values and the essence of your relationship. Assure them that while the format may differ, your commitment to each other and the love you share remain steadfast.

Addressing concerns about missing out on the joyous celebration of a traditional wedding is crucial. Reassure your loved ones that your elopement is not a rejection of their desire to celebrate with you. Instead, it's an invitation to celebrate your love in a more intimate and intentional way. You can even explore opportunities to have post-elopement gatherings or celebrations, where you can share the joy and memories with those who couldn't be present during the ceremony.

One of the most significant concerns may be the fear of missing out on witnessing your union. Loved ones might express a desire to be present during such a momentous occasion. Acknowledge this sentiment and explore ways to involve them, perhaps through live streaming the ceremony or organizing a special gathering where you can share the experience together.

Lastly, some family and friends might worry about the logistics and planning of the elopement. Offer reassurance by sharing your thoughtful planning process, highlighting how you've considered the logistical aspects, such as permits, weather, and accessibility. Provide information about the location, and if possible, involve them in certain aspects of the planning to make them feel connected to the process.

In essence, addressing potential concerns from family and friends is about fostering open and honest communication. By proactively addressing these concerns, you demonstrate respect for their feelings and provide a space for understanding to flourish. Each concern represents an opportunity to deepen the connection and help your loved ones see the beauty and significance of your choice to elope.

Communicating the decision with sensitivity and clarity

When communicating the decision to elope, the way you convey your choice plays a crucial role in shaping the understanding and support of your loved ones. It's essential to approach this communication with sensitivity, clarity, and a genuine expression of your emotions to create a space for open dialogue and shared understanding.

Begin by acknowledging the significance of the conversation. Express that the decision to elope is deeply personal and rooted in your desire for a celebration that authentically reflects your relationship. Setting the tone with sincerity helps your loved ones recognize the authenticity behind your choice.

Choose a suitable setting for this conversation, one that allows for an intimate and focused exchange. Whether it's a family gathering or a one-on-one discussion, ensure that the environment is conducive to open communication. By selecting the right setting, you convey the importance of the conversation and the respect you have for your loved ones' feelings.

As you delve into the discussion, be clear about your motivations. Share the reasons behind your choice to elope, emphasizing the aspects of an intimate celebration that resonate with you and your partner. Whether it's the desire for a deeper connection, the love for nature, or the pursuit of a unique and personal experience, articulate your motivations with authenticity.

Express your emotions openly. Let your loved ones see the joy, excitement, and love that accompany your decision. Sharing your emotional journey helps them connect with the sincerity of your choice and understand the profound meaning it holds for you and your partner.

It's equally important to be prepared for a range of reactions. Some family members or friends may express surprise, while others might readily embrace the idea. Be patient and receptive to their emotions, understanding that each individual may process the information differently. Creating a space where they feel comfortable sharing their thoughts contributes to a more meaningful conversation.

Use language that emphasizes continuity rather than departure. Assure your loved ones that while the format of the celebration may differ, your commitment to your relationships remains unwavering. Reinforce that the elopement is an extension of your love story, crafted to align with your values and desires, rather than a deviation from familial bonds.

Invite your loved ones to be part of the journey in meaningful ways. If there are aspects of the elopement planning they can contribute to, involve them in the process. By creating opportunities for their participation, you reinforce the idea that, despite the intimate nature of the ceremony, they are valued contributors to your celebration.

Be open to questions and concerns, and address them with patience and empathy. Providing clarity on logistical aspects, financial considerations, and the planning process helps alleviate potential uncertainties. By openly sharing your thoughtfulness in the planning process, you demonstrate the care you've taken in ensuring a meaningful and well-prepared celebration.

In conclusion, communicating the decision to elope with sensitivity and clarity is about fostering an atmosphere of understanding and support. By approaching the conversation with authenticity, emotional openness, and a genuine desire to share your joy, you pave the way for your loved ones to connect with the essence of your choice and celebrate this significant moment in your life.

Including Loved Ones

Including loved ones in your elopement journey is a beautiful way to bridge the gap between an intimate celebration and the desire to share your joy with those you cherish. While the decision to elope is often rooted in the desire for a more private experience, finding meaningful ways to involve your loved ones can create lasting memories and strengthen the bonds that matter most.

Firstly, consider the possibility of a pre-elopement celebration or gathering. This could be an opportunity to share your excitement and intentions with close family and friends. Whether it's an intimate dinner, a casual get-together, or a virtual gathering, this pre-celebration allows you to express your love and gratitude while providing loved ones with a chance to share in the joy leading up to your elopement.

Involve your loved ones in the planning process. While the ceremony itself may be an intimate affair, there are numerous aspects of the elopement that family and friends can contribute to. Seek their input on elements such as attire, decor, or even choosing the perfect location. This involvement not only creates a sense of shared responsibility but also allows your loved ones to feel connected to the celebration in a meaningful way.

Consider having a virtual component to your elopement. With the advancements in technology, live streaming the ceremony can bring loved ones from afar into the heart of the celebration. This virtual presence allows them to witness the exchange of vows, share in the joyous moments, and be a part of your special day, even from a distance.

Encourage loved ones to contribute to the celebration in unique ways. This could involve asking family and friends to share well-wishes, readings, or even musical performances that can be incorporated into the ceremony. By giving them an active role, you deepen their connection to the celebration and infuse the ceremony with personalized touches.

Create a shared memory bank. Invite loved ones to contribute photos, videos, or messages that capture the essence of their relationship with you and your partner. Compile these into a digital or physical keepsake that serves as a beautiful testament to the love and support surrounding your elopement.

If feasible, plan a post-elopement celebration. This could be a gathering where you share your elopement experience, exchange stories, and relive the joyous moments with those who were not physically present during the ceremony. Whether it's a casual picnic, a backyard barbecue, or a more formal reception, this post-celebration allows you to extend the joy and share the love with a wider circle.

Keep communication channels open. Actively share updates, insights, and behind-the-scenes glimpses of your elopement journey with loved ones. Regular communication ensures that they feel included and valued throughout the process, fostering a sense of connection even if they are not physically present.

Ultimately, including loved ones in your elopement journey is about finding the delicate balance between the intimacy of the celebration and the desire to share your joy with those who matter most. By thoughtfully integrating your loved ones into various aspects of the elopement experience, you create a celebration that is not only deeply personal but also rich with shared love and memories.

Selecting a small group of guests for an intimate experience

Choosing a small group of guests for your elopement adds a layer of intimacy and meaningful connection to your celebration. While eloping often involves a more private affair, carefully selecting a small group of loved ones to share in the experience can enhance the joy, support, and emotional depth of your special day.

Start by identifying the individuals who hold the closest places in your heart. These could be immediate family members, a select group of friends, or individuals who have played significant roles in your lives. By narrowing down your guest list to those who share a deep connection with you and your partner, you ensure that each attendee contributes to the intimate atmosphere you envision.

Consider the dynamics of your relationships. The goal is to create an atmosphere where every guest feels not just invited but genuinely valued. Think about the connections between your chosen guests, ensuring that they share positive and harmonious relationships with each other. This creates a cohesive and supportive environment during your elopement, where everyone present contributes to the joyous atmosphere.

Engage in open and honest communication with your chosen guests. Share your decision to elope and express why their presence is meaningful to you. By communicating your intentions and feelings, you provide them with a deeper understanding of the significance of their role in your elopement. This transparency fosters a sense of connection and ensures that they feel both honored and involved in your special day.

Consider the logistics of the location and the size of the gathering. Opting for an intimate setting that comfortably accommodates your small group of guests enhances the overall experience. Whether it's a scenic outdoor location or a cozy indoor venue, selecting a space that complements the intimacy of the gathering ensures that every guest feels connected to the celebration.

Personalize the experience for each guest. While the guest list may be small, incorporating personal touches tailored to each individual adds a layer of thoughtfulness. Whether it's personalized notes, small gifts, or specific roles in the ceremony, these gestures demonstrate your appreciation for their presence and contribute to the uniqueness of the experience.

Encourage your guests to play active roles in the celebration. Whether it's through readings, well-wishes, or even participating in symbolic rituals, involving them in the ceremony fosters a sense of shared participation. This engagement not only enriches the overall experience but also reinforces the bonds between you, your partner, and your chosen guests.

Capture the moments. With a small group, there's an opportunity to document the intimate interactions and emotions more closely. Consider having a photographer or videographer who specializes in capturing the nuances of small gatherings. The resulting images and footage become treasured mementos, immortalizing the genuine connections and emotions shared during your elopement.

Plan post-elopement activities. Following the ceremony, arrange for a small gathering or meal where you can celebrate with your guests in a relaxed setting. This provides an opportunity for everyone to share stories, express their joy, and create lasting memories together.

In conclusion, selecting a small group of guests for an intimate elopement experience involves thoughtful consideration of your relationships, open communication, and personalization. By curating a guest list comprised of individuals who share deep connections with you and your partner, you create an environment where every presence adds to the richness of your celebration.

Involving family and friends in pre-wedding adventures

Involving family and friends in pre-wedding adventures can be a delightful way to share the joy and anticipation leading up to your elopement. While eloping often conjures images of intimate moments between partners, extending the celebration to include loved ones in pre-wedding activities can enhance the overall experience and create cherished memories for everyone involved.

Start by gauging the interest and availability of your family and friends. Share your plans for pre-wedding adventures and inquire about their willingness to join. Consider their schedules, preferences, and any logistical constraints to ensure that the activities align with everyone's comfort and availability.

Choose activities that cater to various interests and fitness levels. Whether it's a scenic hike, a leisurely bike ride, or a relaxed picnic, selecting adventures that accommodate a range of preferences ensures that everyone can participate comfortably. This inclusivity fosters a sense of togetherness and allows each participant to contribute their unique energy to the pre-wedding festivities.

Highlight the significance of these pre-wedding adventures. Express to your family and friends how their presence during these moments adds a layer of joy and shared experiences to your elopement journey. Emphasize the opportunity for bonding and creating lasting memories that extend beyond the wedding day itself.

Incorporate personalized touches into the activities. Consider including elements that hold sentimental value for you and your loved ones. Whether it's revisiting a meaningful location, incorporating favorite foods, or engaging in activities that reflect shared interests, these personalized touches add depth and significance to the pre-wedding adventures.

Create opportunities for connection and conversation. Pre-wedding adventures provide a relaxed and informal setting for your family and friends to interact and get to know each other better. Facilitate conversations, encourage shared laughter, and allow the natural flow of connection to unfold, fostering a sense of camaraderie among all participants.

Document the moments. While the elopement itself may be an intimate affair, capturing the pre-wedding adventures ensures that the shared joy and anticipation are preserved. Consider having a photographer or designated documenter to capture candid moments, group photos, and the genuine interactions that unfold during these activities.

Coordinate logistics thoughtfully. From transportation to the choice of activities, ensure that the logistics are well-planned and considerate of everyone involved. Clear communication about the schedule, expectations, and any necessary preparations ensures that everyone can fully engage and enjoy the pre-wedding adventures.

Extend gratitude and appreciation. Throughout the pre-wedding adventures, express your gratitude to your family and friends for being part of these special moments. Acknowledge the role each person plays in contributing to the joyous atmosphere and building beautiful memories together.

In conclusion, involving family and friends in pre-wedding adventures is a wonderful way to extend the celebration and create shared memories leading up to your elopement. By considering their interests, highlighting the significance of these moments, and incorporating personalized touches, you contribute to a joyful and inclusive experience for everyone involved.

Celebrating with a Wider Circle

Celebrating with a wider circle involves sharing the joy of your elopement with friends and family who may not be physically present but are an essential part of your support system. While eloping often implies an intimate ceremony, there are numerous ways to include a broader community in the celebration, making it a collective experience that transcends geographical boundaries.

Start by setting the tone for inclusivity. Communicate your elopement plans openly with your wider circle, expressing your desire to celebrate this significant moment with everyone, regardless of their physical location. Use digital platforms, such as social media, video calls, or live streaming, to create a virtual space for your loved ones to join in the festivities.

Consider organizing a virtual pre-celebration. Host an online gathering where friends and family can share their well-wishes, anecdotes, and blessings leading up to the elopement. This allows you to connect with your wider circle in a meaningful way and ensures that they feel included in the joyous occasion.

Share the journey in real-time. Utilize social media platforms to provide updates and behind-the-scenes glimpses into your elopement preparations. Whether it's posting about scouting the perfect location, selecting attire, or engaging in pre-wedding adventures, sharing these moments virtually invites your wider circle to participate in the excitement.

Create a digital guestbook. Encourage friends and family to send their best wishes, advice, or even short video messages. Compile these heartfelt contributions into a digital guestbook that serves as a lasting memento of the love and support surrounding your elopement. This not only involves your wider circle but also provides a tangible representation of their presence.

Organize a post-elopement virtual celebration. After the elopement, host a virtual reception or celebration where you can share highlights, exchange stories, and express your gratitude to your wider circle. This post-elopement gathering allows you to reminisce about the day, showcase photographs, and celebrate the union with those who couldn't be physically present.

Consider sending elopement announcements. Share the joy of your union by sending personalized elopement announcements to your wider circle. Include a heartfelt message, a few select photos, and details about how they can access additional content or participate in virtual celebrations. This thoughtful gesture ensures that even those who couldn't be present physically feel connected to your special day.

Encourage participation through social media challenges. Create a unique hashtag for your elopement and invite friends and family to participate in social media challenges, such as sharing their favorite memories with you or recreating a cherished moment. This not only fosters engagement but also creates a sense of shared celebration across distances.

Express gratitude and acknowledge their presence. Throughout the elopement journey and beyond, express your gratitude to your wider circle for their love and support. Acknowledge the role they play in making your celebration complete, even from afar, and emphasize how their presence, virtual or otherwise, contributes to the joyous atmosphere.

In summary, celebrating with a wider circle involves leveraging digital platforms and creative approaches to include friends and family who may not be physically present in your elopement. From virtual pre-celebrations to post-elopement gatherings, these initiatives foster a sense of community, ensuring that your wider circle remains an integral part of the joyous occasion.

Planning post-elopement celebrations for a larger audience

Planning post-elopement celebrations for a larger audience involves thoughtful considerations to ensure that everyone who wishes to share in your joy can do so in a meaningful way. While eloping may be an intimate affair, extending the celebration beyond the actual ceremony allows you to include a larger audience in the festivities.

Start by setting the stage for a grand celebration. Communicate your post-elopement plans to your wider circle, expressing your eagerness to continue the festivities with them. Share the date and details of the virtual celebration, making it clear that you want to include as many friends and family members as possible in the joyous occasion.

Choose a virtual platform that suits the scale of your celebration. Platforms like Zoom, Google Meet, or other video conferencing tools offer features that accommodate a larger audience. Ensure that the chosen platform supports interactive elements, such as live chats, reactions, and the ability for participants to share their own video feeds.

Consider a virtual reception with a personal touch. Instead of a traditional reception, organize a virtual gathering that captures the essence of post-elopement celebrations. Include elements like a virtual toast, a shared playlist, or even a digital dance floor where participants can join in from their own locations. This creates a festive atmosphere and allows everyone to feel connected despite the physical distance.

Incorporate interactive elements to engage the audience. Plan activities that involve your wider circle in the celebration. This could include virtual games, trivia related to your relationship, or even a live Q&A session where friends and family can ask questions and share their well-wishes. By fostering interaction, you create a sense of shared participation.

Share highlights of the elopement day. Create a visually appealing presentation or slideshow featuring the key moments of your elopement. Showcase photographs, video clips, and anecdotes that provide a glimpse into the beauty of the ceremony. This not only allows your larger audience to witness the magic but also creates a shared experience.

Send out digital invitations with a personal touch. Craft digital invitations that reflect the style and theme of your elopement. Include a heartfelt message expressing your desire to celebrate with a wider audience and provide clear instructions on how to join the virtual festivities. Personalize the invitations to make each recipient feel special.

Encourage participation through virtual contributions. Invite friends and family to contribute to the virtual celebration by sharing their own videos, messages, or well-wishes. Create a designated space for these contributions, such as a shared online platform or a collaborative document, allowing everyone to actively participate in the joyous occasion.

Consider time zone differences when planning. Since your larger audience may be scattered across different time zones, be mindful of scheduling the virtual celebration at a time that accommodates the majority. Consider alternatives, such as recording key segments for those who might be in different time zones, ensuring that everyone can engage with the celebration.

Express gratitude and make it inclusive. Throughout the virtual celebration, express gratitude to your larger audience for being a part of the post-elopement festivities. Acknowledge their presence, share the love, and emphasize how their participation makes the celebration complete. By fostering inclusivity, you create a sense of connection and shared joy.

In summary, planning post-elopement celebrations for a larger audience involves leveraging virtual platforms, incorporating interactive elements, and ensuring that everyone feels included in the joyous occasion. From a virtual reception to interactive activities, these considerations make the celebration accessible and engaging for a broader circle of friends and family.

Balancing intimate elopement with broader social connections

Balancing an intimate elopement with broader social connections requires thoughtful consideration to ensure that your extended circle feels acknowledged and valued while preserving the intimate essence of your elopement. Striking this balance allows you to share your joy with a larger audience without compromising the personal and intimate nature of your special day.

Acknowledge the dual nature of your celebration. Begin by acknowledging that your elopement was intentionally intimate, emphasizing the personal significance of sharing this moment with a select few. Clearly express your gratitude for the presence and support of those who were part of the intimate ceremony, highlighting the deep emotional connection you share with them.

Communicate openly about your elopement choices. Share the reasons behind your decision to elope intimately, emphasizing that it was a choice made to prioritize the depth and authenticity of your commitment. By providing context for your decision, you help others understand the thought and intentionality that went into creating a meaningful and intimate experience.

Highlight the value of personal connections. Emphasize the importance of personal connections and how the intimate setting allowed for a more profound exchange of vows and emotions. Make it clear that the smaller gathering facilitated a unique and personal experience that may not have been possible in a larger, more traditional setting.

Organize separate celebrations with different purposes. Consider organizing distinct celebrations to cater to different aspects of your social connections. Host a small, intimate gathering for those who were part of the elopement, where you can reminisce about the special day and share personal anecdotes. Simultaneously, plan a broader celebration for friends and family who were not present at the elopement, focusing on joyous and inclusive moments.

Share the joy through storytelling. Craft a compelling narrative that captures the essence of your elopement, using storytelling to convey the emotions, scenery, and significance of the day. Whether through written accounts, photographs, or video presentations, create a story that can be easily shared with your broader social circle, allowing them to connect with the essence of your celebration.

Utilize digital platforms for sharing. Leverage digital platforms to share your elopement journey with a wider audience. Create a dedicated website, blog, or social media platform where you can document your elopement story, share photographs, and express your feelings. This allows friends and family who were not physically present to experience the magic of your day in a virtual yet meaningful way.

Host virtual gatherings for broader connections. Organize virtual gatherings or online events that bring together your extended social circle. This could include a virtual party, video call, or live-streamed celebration where you express your love and gratitude to a broader audience. Incorporate elements that foster connection and allow everyone to participate in the joyous occasion.

Express openness to future celebrations. Let your broader social circle know that while the elopement was an intimate affair, you are open to future celebrations or gatherings. This communicates that your commitment to sharing your joy extends beyond the elopement day, creating anticipation for future opportunities to come together and celebrate.

In summary, balancing an intimate elopement with broader social connections involves clear communication, acknowledging the significance of personal connections, and finding creative ways to share the joy with a larger audience. By combining heartfelt storytelling, digital sharing, and separate celebrations, you can strike a harmonious balance that honors both the intimacy of your elopement and the desire to include a broader social circle in your celebration of love.

Chapter 9: Budget-Friendly Outdoor Elopements

Welcome to Chapter 9: Budget-Friendly Outdoor Elopements. In this chapter, we embark on a journey that proves that a magical outdoor elopement need not break the bank. The allure of saying "I do" amidst nature's grandeur can be achieved with thoughtful planning, resourcefulness, and a touch of creativity. Whether you're dreaming of a mountaintop ceremony, a beachside exchange of vows, or a forest elopement, we'll explore practical strategies to make your outdoor celebration both unforgettable and budget-conscious.

In a world where the cost of weddings can sometimes overshadow the true essence of the celebration, opting for a budget-friendly outdoor elopement allows you to prioritize what truly matters – the love and commitment you share with your partner. This chapter is designed to guide you through a range of cost-effective considerations, from choosing the perfect outdoor location to thoughtfully curating your ceremony and reception elements without compromising on the magic of the moment.

Discover how to make savvy decisions when it comes to selecting your venue, decor, attire, and more, ensuring that every aspect of your outdoor elopement aligns with your vision while staying within your budgetary constraints. We'll delve into creative alternatives, DIY approaches, and strategic planning that empower you to achieve the wedding of your dreams without a hefty price tag.

Whether you're working with a modest budget or simply prefer a more economical approach to your wedding celebration, this chapter is your companion in navigating the world of budget-friendly outdoor elopements. Let's embark on this adventure together, proving that love knows no financial boundaries and that the beauty of nature can be the perfect backdrop for a celebration that's both magical and mindful of your budget.

Cost-Saving Strategies

As you venture into the realm of planning a budget-friendly outdoor elopement, it's essential to adopt a strategic mindset, exploring various avenues to curate a celebration that is both cost-effective and enchanting. In this section, we'll delve into a myriad of cost-saving strategies that empower you to make informed decisions while staying true to your vision.

First and foremost, consider the timing of your elopement. Opting for off-peak seasons or weekdays can significantly reduce venue costs, as many outdoor locations offer discounts during less popular times. This not only stretches your budget but also provides a more intimate experience as you share your vows surrounded by the tranquility of nature.

When selecting an outdoor venue, explore public spaces or nature reserves that may offer lower rental fees compared to private venues. Many public parks and natural settings allow elopements with minimal or no fees, letting you redirect those savings toward other aspects of your celebration.

Embrace the DIY spirit when it comes to decor. Nature itself is a breathtaking backdrop, and simple, homemade touches can enhance the ambiance without breaking the bank. Consider crafting your own ceremony arch using locally sourced materials, repurposing items from thrift stores, or utilizing natural elements like wildflowers and branches for centerpieces.

Another key aspect to consider is attire. Explore budget-friendly options for your wedding attire, perhaps opting for off-the-rack dresses, second-hand finds, or even non-traditional outfits that can be repurposed for future occasions. This not only contributes to a more sustainable approach but also allows you to allocate more of your budget to experiences rather than material costs.

For the reception or post-elopement celebration, think creatively about catering. Instead of a traditional sit-down dinner, consider a picnic-style gathering with locally sourced, simple fare. Food trucks or catering services specializing in casual dining can provide delicious options at a fraction of the cost of a formal meal.

Additionally, embrace the power of digital communication. Invitations, save-the-dates, and even thank-you cards can be designed and sent online, reducing printing and postage costs. This not only aligns with a modern, eco-friendly approach but also allows you to redirect funds to elements that will truly enhance your elopement experience.

By incorporating these cost-saving strategies, you can navigate the planning process with confidence, knowing that your budget-friendly outdoor elopement is a testament to resourcefulness and thoughtful decision-making. Remember, the true magic of your celebration lies in the love you share and the natural beauty that surrounds you, proving that a memorable elopement doesn't have to come with a hefty price tag.

Tips for eloping on a budget without compromising the experience

Embarking on the journey of eloping on a budget doesn't mean sacrificing the magic and significance of your celebration. In fact, it's an opportunity to infuse creativity and thoughtfulness into every aspect of your elopement. Let's explore some invaluable tips to ensure that your budget-friendly elopement remains a cherished and meaningful experience.

First and foremost, prioritize what matters most to you as a couple. Identify the elements that hold sentimental value and focus your budget on those aspects.

Whether it's the perfect outdoor location, a photographer to capture those precious moments, or a special detail in your attire, allocating your budget wisely allows you to invest in the elements that will make your elopement uniquely yours.

Consider an intimate guest list. While eloping often implies a smaller gathering, be intentional about who you invite. Limiting the guest count not only creates a more personal and meaningful experience but also reduces costs associated with catering, seating, and other logistics.

Flexibility is key when it comes to scheduling. Explore weekdays or off-peak seasons for your elopement, as many vendors and venues offer discounted rates during these times. This flexibility not only stretches your budget but also allows for a more serene and private experience in your chosen outdoor setting.

Explore non-traditional venues. Public parks, beaches, or nature reserves often have minimal or no venue fees, providing a stunning backdrop without the hefty price tag. Be open to unconventional yet enchanting locations that resonate with your vision.

Embrace the do-it-yourself ethos for decor and details. Crafting your own ceremony arch, designing simple yet elegant centerpieces, or repurposing items from thrift stores can add a personal touch without breaking the bank. Engaging in creative, hands-on projects also makes the process more enjoyable and reflective of your unique style.

When it comes to attire, think beyond traditional wedding outfits. Consider off-the-rack dresses, second-hand finds, or even outfits you can repurpose for future occasions. This not only aligns with a budget-friendly approach but also allows for more versatile and sustainable choices.

Digital invitations and communication can significantly cut costs. Explore online platforms for sending invitations, save-the-dates, and thank-you cards. This not only reduces printing and postage expenses but also aligns with a modern, eco-friendly approach.

Finally, communicate openly with your vendors. Many professionals are willing to work within a budget, especially if they understand the significance of your elopement. Negotiate and discuss options, ensuring that you receive quality services that enhance your experience without straining your finances.

In essence, eloping on a budget is about making intentional choices that reflect your values and priorities. By infusing creativity, flexibility, and thoughtful decision-making into the planning process, you can create a budget-friendly elopement that is both magical and memorable. Remember, it's not about the price tag; it's about the love you share and the meaningful moments you create together.

Identifying cost-effective alternatives for various elements

In the pursuit of a budget-friendly outdoor elopement, identifying cost-effective alternatives for various elements becomes a delightful and creative endeavor. From the venue to decor and everything in between, exploring alternative options ensures that you can craft a celebration that is both affordable and uniquely yours.

Let's start with the venue, a pivotal aspect of any elopement. Instead of traditional venues that may come with hefty price tags, consider public spaces, parks, or nature reserves. Many of these locations offer breathtaking backdrops without the burden of venue fees. Public spaces not only provide a picturesque setting but also often carry sentimental value, adding an extra layer of significance to your celebration.

When it comes to decor, think outside the conventional wedding box. Opt for cost-effective alternatives such as repurposing thrifted items or crafting your own decor. DIY projects not only contribute to a more personalized atmosphere but also allow you to infuse your unique style into the celebration. For example, creating a simple yet elegant ceremony arch using affordable materials can serve as a focal point without straining your budget.

Consider alternative options for seating arrangements. Instead of renting chairs, opt for blankets, cushions, or even hay bales for a rustic touch. Embrace the casual and intimate vibe of an outdoor setting, where unconventional seating choices can add charm and character to your elopement.

Catering costs can be a significant portion of the budget, but there are creative ways to manage expenses without compromising on quality. Explore local and affordable catering options, such as food trucks or casual dining services. You can also consider a potluck-style celebration, where guests contribute dishes, adding a communal and heartfelt touch to the dining experience.

Photography is a non-negotiable element for many couples, as it captures the essence of the day for years to come. Instead of hiring a high-end photographer, research local talent or emerging photographers who may offer more budget-friendly packages. Many photographers are willing to work within varying budget constraints, especially when they connect with the unique vision of your elopement.

Attire costs can also be managed creatively. Consider off-the-rack dresses, second-hand finds, or outfits that can be repurposed for future occasions. Many couples find joy in choosing attire that aligns with their personal style while remaining mindful of the budget.

Transportation is another aspect where cost-effective alternatives can be explored. Instead of renting expensive vehicles, consider using your own car or arranging a ride-sharing service. This not only reduces costs but also adds a personal touch to your journey.

Ultimately, identifying cost-effective alternatives for various elements of your elopement is about embracing the spirit of resourcefulness and creativity. It's an opportunity to curate a celebration that reflects your values and priorities without the burden of unnecessary expenses. By thinking outside the traditional wedding norms, you can craft a budget-friendly elopement that is authentically yours and filled with meaningful moments.

DIY Decor and Details

Delving into the world of DIY decor and details is an exhilarating journey that not only infuses your outdoor elopement with a personalized touch but also allows you to express your creativity in unique ways. From centerpieces to signage, embracing a do-it-yourself approach can transform your celebration into a canvas of meaningful and crafted moments.

Let's start with centerpieces, focal points that add charm to your elopement space. Instead of opting for costly floral arrangements, consider creating your own using seasonal and local blooms. Gather inspiration from nature, and craft simple but elegant arrangements in mismatched vases or repurposed containers. Incorporating elements like branches, pinecones, or wildflowers can add a rustic and organic vibe to your tables.

Personalized signage is another DIY detail that can guide and enchant your guests. Craft your own welcome sign, ceremony programs, or directional signs using materials that resonate with your outdoor setting. Wooden boards, chalkboards, or even repurposed window panes can serve as charming canvases for your handwritten or calligraphed messages.

For a whimsical touch, consider crafting your own ceremony arch or backdrop. Choose materials that align with your theme and setting, whether it's driftwood for a beach elopement or reclaimed wood for a rustic affair. Adorn the structure with fabric, flowers, or greenery to create a captivating focal point for your vows.

Table settings provide an opportunity to showcase your DIY prowess while adding a personalized touch to your dining experience. Consider crafting your own place cards, napkin rings, or table runners. Utilize natural elements like leaves, twine, or recycled paper for a cohesive and eco-friendly aesthetic.

DIY favors offer a heartfelt way to express gratitude to your guests. Consider creating small tokens that reflect your personality as a couple and tie into the outdoor theme. Handmade candles, personalized seed packets, or locally sourced treats are charming options that guests can cherish as mementos of your special day.

Enhance the ambiance with handmade lighting elements. Craft your own lanterns, fairy lights, or candle holders to illuminate the evening festivities. Utilize mason jars, repurposed wine bottles, or even simple string lights to create a warm and inviting atmosphere.

Capture candid moments with a DIY photo booth, complete with handmade props and backdrops. This interactive element not only adds a touch of fun to your celebration but also provides guests with the opportunity to create lasting memories.

When it comes to DIY decor and details, the key is to infuse your personality and style into every element. Whether you're repurposing items you already own or embarking on crafting adventures, the result will be a celebration that feels authentically yours. Embrace the joy of creating, and let the DIY process become an integral part of your elopement story, filled with love, creativity, and meaningful details crafted by your own hands.

Creating personalized decor on a budget

Crafting personalized decor on a budget is a delightful challenge that allows you to infuse your outdoor elopement with unique and meaningful touches without breaking the bank. With a touch of creativity and resourcefulness, you can create a personalized ambiance that resonates with your love story and the natural surroundings.

One of the most cost-effective ways to personalize your decor is through repurposing everyday items. Look around your home for objects that hold sentimental value or reflect your shared interests. Vintage books, antique frames, or family heirlooms can become charming decor elements that tell a story. Embrace the beauty of imperfections and create a curated collection that mirrors your journey as a couple.

Consider incorporating elements from your love story into the decor. If you met at a coffee shop, for example, collect coffee cans or mugs to use as vases or candle holders. If you share a love for travel, utilize maps or globes in your decor. These personal touches not only add character to the setting but also invite guests to connect with the narrative of your relationship.

Personalized signage is a budget-friendly way to share your story and guide guests throughout the celebration. Craft your own welcome signs, directional signs, or table numbers using materials like chalkboards, wooden boards, or even repurposed window frames. Handwritten messages or calligraphy add an intimate and personal touch.

Photographs are powerful storytellers, and incorporating them into your decor is both budget-friendly and sentimental. Create a timeline of your relationship by displaying photos from significant moments on a string of twine or pinned to a vintage ladder. This not only adds a personal touch to your decor but also invites guests to reminisce with you.

Explore nature for budget-friendly decor inspiration. Collect pinecones, rocks, or fallen leaves to incorporate into your centerpieces, table settings, or as part of a backdrop. Consider utilizing natural elements like twigs, branches, or driftwood to craft rustic decor pieces that seamlessly blend with the outdoor environment.

Repurposing and upcycling materials is a sustainable and cost-effective approach to personalized decor. Visit thrift stores, garage sales, or local flea markets to discover hidden gems that can be transformed into one-of-a-kind decor pieces. Old windows, wooden crates, or vintage lanterns can be repurposed to add character to your celebration.

For a touch of whimsy, consider crafting your own personalized bunting or banners. Use fabric remnants, burlap, or even old linens to create charming flags that can be adorned with meaningful quotes, dates, or symbols. String these across the ceremony or reception space for a budget-friendly and visually appealing decor element.

The key to creating personalized decor on a budget is to infuse each element with intention and meaning. By leveraging your creativity and resourcefulness, you can transform ordinary items into extraordinary expressions of your love. Personalized decor not only adds warmth and authenticity to your elopement but also creates an immersive experience that resonates with you, your partner, and your cherished guests.

Incorporating DIY elements into the overall aesthetic

Incorporating DIY elements into the overall aesthetic of your outdoor elopement is a fantastic way to infuse the celebration with your unique personality and creativity. Not only does it add a personal touch, but it also allows you to create a cohesive and visually stunning environment that reflects your love story.

When embracing a DIY approach to your elopement decor, consider the overall theme and style you want to convey. Whether it's rustic, bohemian, vintage, or a blend of styles, your DIY elements should harmonize with the chosen aesthetic. Consistency in design will contribute to a polished and well-thought-out ambiance.

One of the most impactful ways to incorporate DIY elements is through handmade centerpieces. Get creative with materials like mason jars, recycled bottles, or wooden crates to craft unique containers for flowers or candles. Personalize each centerpiece by adding touches like lace, twine, or hand-painted details that align with your chosen theme.

Consider crafting your own ceremony backdrop or arch. Utilize materials such as reclaimed wood, bamboo, or copper pipes to construct a frame, and then adorn it with fabrics, flowers, or greenery that complements the natural surroundings. Personalize the backdrop further by incorporating meaningful elements such as photographs or handcrafted signage.

DIY signage adds a charming and personal touch to your elopement. Create directional signs, welcome boards, or even a schedule of events using chalkboards, wooden boards, or repurposed frames. Handwriting or calligraphy adds an intimate feel, and you can experiment with different fonts and styles to match your chosen aesthetic.

For an eco-friendly and budget-conscious approach, consider crafting your own confetti or petal toss. Collect fallen leaves, use a heart-shaped hole punch on recycled paper, or dry flowers from your garden. Place these DIY confetti in biodegradable bags or containers for guests to grab before the ceremony, creating a whimsical and environmentally conscious moment.

Incorporating DIY elements into your table settings can elevate the overall aesthetic. Craft your own place cards using natural materials like leaves or wooden slices. Personalize napkin rings or holders with small trinkets or charms that reflect your personalities. DIY details on the tablescape create an intimate and thoughtful atmosphere for you and your guests.

When it comes to lighting, DIY lanterns or candle holders can add a magical touch to the ambiance.

Create your own lanterns using mason jars, twine, and tea lights. Hang these lanterns from trees or place them along pathways for a romantic and enchanting glow.

In summary, incorporating DIY elements into the overall aesthetic of your outdoor elopement allows you to infuse the celebration with your unique style and story. From handmade centerpieces to personalized signage, each DIY detail contributes to a cohesive and visually stunning environment. Embrace the creative process, and let your DIY elements speak to the authenticity of your love and the beauty of your chosen outdoor setting.

Affordable Adventure Options

Embracing the spirit of adventure doesn't have to come with a hefty price tag. In fact, there are countless affordable options to infuse excitement and thrill into your outdoor elopement, making it a memorable and budget-friendly celebration.

Consider exploring nearby hiking trails or nature reserves for your adventure. Many locations offer stunning landscapes, from majestic mountains to serene lakeshores, providing a picturesque backdrop for your elopement without the need for expensive venue fees. Research the trails in advance, choosing one that aligns with your fitness level and desired scenery.

Another affordable adventure option is opting for a sunrise or sunset elopement. Nature's golden hours offer breathtaking lighting and a romantic atmosphere, creating an enchanting backdrop for your vows. Choose a location with a clear view of the horizon, allowing you to exchange your vows as the sun paints the sky in hues of pink and gold.

For couples seeking a touch of adrenaline, consider incorporating adventure activities into your elopement day. Many outdoor destinations offer affordable options such as zip-lining, canoeing, or hot air balloon rides. These activities not only add an adventurous flair to your celebration but also create lasting memories of a day filled with excitement.

Explore budget-friendly accommodation options to enhance the adventure aspect of your elopement. Look into campsites, cabins, or unique Airbnb rentals near your chosen outdoor location. Camping under the stars or waking up in a cozy cabin can add an extra layer of romance and adventure to your elopement without breaking the bank.

Engage in local experiences that capture the essence of your chosen destination. Whether it's attending a cultural event, exploring a charming town, or participating in a community celebration, these experiences can infuse your elopement with a sense of place and local charm. Many of these activities are often free or have a minimal cost, making them accessible to various budgets.

If you're considering a beach elopement, take advantage of the natural beauty that the shoreline provides. Plan your ceremony during low tide to reveal more of the beach, creating a stunning and expansive backdrop. Alternatively, consider a beach bonfire celebration, where you and your loved ones can gather around a fire pit, sharing stories and toasting marshmallows.

Incorporate DIY adventure elements into your celebration. Craft your own treasure hunt or scavenger hunt for you and your guests to explore the surrounding area. Include meaningful locations or landmarks that hold significance to your relationship, creating an interactive and personalized adventure.

In conclusion, there are numerous affordable adventure options to infuse excitement and thrill into your outdoor elopement. Whether it's exploring hiking trails, embracing sunrise or sunset ceremonies, incorporating adventure activities, or engaging in local experiences, the key is to embrace the natural beauty of your chosen location and create a celebration that reflects your unique love story. By exploring these budget-friendly options, you can elevate your elopement into an unforgettable adventure without breaking the bank.

Budget-friendly outdoor activities and experiences

Navigating the realms of budget-friendly outdoor activities and experiences can be an exciting journey, allowing couples to create unforgettable moments without a significant financial burden. The key lies in exploring the beauty of nature while keeping an eye on cost-effective alternatives that amplify the joy of your elopement.

One of the most accessible and budget-friendly outdoor activities is embarking on a scenic hike. Choose trails that offer stunning vistas, whether it's a mountaintop with panoramic views or a trail leading to a hidden waterfall. Hiking not only provides a sense of adventure but also an opportunity for intimate moments surrounded by nature's grandeur.

Picnics are a classic and affordable way to enjoy the outdoors. Select a picturesque spot, pack a basket with your favorite snacks and refreshments, and revel in a delightful meal together. Whether it's a sun-dappled meadow, a quiet beach, or a charming park, a picnic allows you to savor the simplicity of nature while creating cherished memories.

Consider incorporating a photo scavenger hunt into your elopement day. This budget-friendly and entertaining activity encourages exploration and adds an element of fun to your celebration. Create a list of specific shots or moments you want to capture, encouraging you and your guests to discover the surroundings while documenting the joyous occasion.

Stargazing can turn your elopement evening into a magical experience. If your celebration extends into the night, find a location away from city lights, spread out a blanket, and marvel at the celestial display overhead. Bring along a telescope or use stargazing apps to identify constellations, adding a celestial touch to your outdoor adventure.

Beachcombing is a budget-friendly and whimsical activity for couples drawn to coastal elopements. Wander along the shoreline, collecting seashells, driftwood, or unique stones as keepsakes from your special day. The rhythmic sound of waves and the soft touch of sand underfoot create a serene backdrop for these simple yet meaningful moments.

Host a simple and intimate bonfire. Many beaches and camping sites allow small fires, providing an atmospheric setting for post-elopement celebrations. Gather around the fire, share stories, and enjoy the warmth as you bask in the glow of the flames. Roasting marshmallows and making s'mores can add a delightful touch to this budget-friendly outdoor experience.

Artistic pursuits like plein air painting or sketching offer a creative and budget-friendly way to capture the essence of your elopement location. Pack some art supplies and unleash your creativity amidst the natural beauty that surrounds you. This personalized artwork can serve as a lasting memento of your special day.

In summary, there are numerous budget-friendly outdoor activities and experiences that couples can explore to enhance their elopement. From scenic hikes and picnics to photo scavenger hunts and stargazing, each activity adds a unique layer to your celebration without straining your budget. By embracing the simplicity and beauty of these experiences, you can create an elopement that feels both authentic and memorable.

Exploring cost-effective adventure options for the elopement itinerary

Embarking on an elopement doesn't mean sacrificing the thrill of adventure. In fact, it opens the door to a world of cost-effective and exciting options that can be seamlessly integrated into your elopement itinerary. From heart-pounding activities to more serene explorations, there are myriad adventure options that won't break the bank.

Consider beginning your adventure-filled day with a sunrise hike. Many natural locations offer breathtaking sunrise views, and a morning hike can infuse your elopement with a sense of renewal and new beginnings. Witnessing the first light of day together creates a magical start to your celebration without adding significant costs.

For water enthusiasts, kayaking or canoeing can be a budget-friendly adventure option. Seek out a serene lake, river, or coastal area, rent kayaks or canoes, and paddle your way through the tranquil waters. This activity not only provides a sense of seclusion but also an intimate connection with nature as you navigate the waterways together.

Thrill-seeking couples might explore rock climbing or bouldering as a cost-effective adventure option. Many outdoor destinations offer accessible climbing spots suitable for beginners, and local climbing gyms often provide affordable rental equipment and introductory lessons. Climbing together can be a metaphor for overcoming challenges, making it a symbolic and adventurous choice.

Mountain biking is an exhilarating adventure option that combines outdoor exploration with a dose of adrenaline. Seek out local trails, whether they are gentle paths or more challenging routes, and embark on a biking adventure through the natural landscape. This activity allows you to cover more ground while immersing yourselves in the beauty of the surroundings.

Geocaching offers a unique and budget-friendly way to add an element of treasure hunting to your elopement day. Utilize GPS coordinates to locate hidden caches in your chosen outdoor location. Each discovery becomes a shared accomplishment, and geocaching provides an interactive and adventurous element to your celebration.

Hot air ballooning may seem like a luxury, but there are often affordable options available, especially in regions known for their scenic landscapes. Soaring above the earth in a balloon provides a breathtaking perspective, and some companies offer budget-friendly rates for shared rides, allowing you to experience the magic of flight without a hefty price tag.

If your elopement location includes bodies of water, paddleboarding can be a serene and budget-friendly adventure. Many coastal and lakeside areas offer paddleboard rentals, allowing you to peacefully glide across the water and take in the beauty of your surroundings. It's a tranquil yet adventurous activity that encourages connection with nature.

In conclusion, exploring cost-effective adventure options for your elopement itinerary opens the door to a world of possibilities. From sunrise hikes and kayaking to rock climbing and geocaching, there are numerous ways to infuse your celebration with a sense of adventure without exceeding your budget. These activities not only create unforgettable moments but also enhance the overall experience of your special day.

Chapter 10: Post-Elopement Reflection and Integration

Chapter 10: Post-Elopement Reflection and Integration

As the echoes of your heartfelt vows and the rustle of the leaves settle, and you find yourselves basking in the afterglow of your outdoor elopement, a new chapter begins – one of reflection, integration, and the weaving of this unique experience into the fabric of your lives. Chapter 10 is a guide to navigating the days and weeks that follow, a gentle exploration of the introspective moments that help you embrace the significance of your decision to elope.

In the aftermath of the elopement adventure, it's common to experience a whirlwind of emotions. Excitement, contentment, and perhaps a tinge of post-celebration blues may accompany you as you step into the routine of daily life. This chapter is designed to be your companion during this transition, offering insights into the art of reflection and the practical aspects of integrating the profound experience of your elopement into your ongoing journey together.

Reflecting on your elopement is not just about looking back; it's about understanding the impact of this intentional choice on your relationship. We'll explore the ways in which the memories of your outdoor celebration can be cherished and how the lessons learned during the planning and execution can contribute to the growth of your partnership.

Integration involves seamlessly blending the elopement experience into the broader tapestry of your lives. From sharing your elopement story with loved ones to creating traditions that honor your commitment, this chapter guides you through the steps that transform a single day into a lasting, cherished memory that continues to shape your relationship.

So, as you turn the pages of Chapter 10, embrace the reflective journey that follows the crescendo of your elopement. Whether you're savoring quiet moments together, sharing memories with friends and family, or contemplating the many adventures that lie ahead, this chapter is here to accompany you as you navigate the profound and beautiful landscape of post-elopement reflection and integration.

Reflecting on the Experience

In the gentle embrace of post-elopement tranquility, it's only natural to embark on a reflective journey, savoring the essence of the experience that unfolded amid the beauty of nature. As you immerse yourselves in the memories of your outdoor celebration, take a moment to reflect on the intricate tapestry of emotions, the vows exchanged under the open sky, and the unique journey that brought you to this significant day.

Reflection isn't just about revisiting the picturesque scenes or recounting the details of the ceremony; it's a more profound exploration of the impact of your elopement on the very fabric of your relationship. Consider the promises you made, the laughter shared, and the quiet moments that held the weight of your commitment. Reflect on how the natural setting became an integral part of your story, infusing it with a timeless and authentic charm.

Allow yourselves the space to appreciate the decisions you made together, the hurdles you overcame during the planning process, and the joy that enveloped you on the day of your elopement. Whether it was an intimate exchange of vows by a cascading waterfall or a serene ceremony on a sunlit meadow, reflect on how the chosen setting resonated with your connection and added a unique chapter to your shared history.

During this reflective journey, consider documenting your thoughts and emotions. Write a letter to each other, capturing the nuances of what this day meant and continues to mean for your relationship. In the midst of your musings, you might discover newfound depths to your bond, strengthening the foundation you've built through the intentional choice of an outdoor elopement.

Reflection also provides an opportunity to acknowledge the growth and resilience you've cultivated as a couple. Celebrate the shared victories, the compromises made, and the unwavering support you've offered one another. In the quiet moments of contemplation, you may find that the beauty of your elopement extends beyond the visual appeal; it resides in the shared laughter, the tender glances, and the unspoken understanding that binds you together.

As you reflect on the experience, consider how your elopement fits into the broader narrative of your lives. It's not merely a standalone event but a significant chapter in a story that continues to unfold. The memories forged amid nature's embrace are threads that weave seamlessly into the ongoing tapestry of your relationship, creating a narrative that is uniquely yours.

Processing emotions and memories after the elopement

In the aftermath of the joyous whirlwind that is your elopement, it's natural to find yourself immersed in a myriad of emotions. Processing these feelings is an essential part of the post-celebration journey, allowing you to fully grasp the significance of the memories you've just created together.

Emotions after an elopement can be as diverse as the colors of a sunset, ranging from sheer elation and contentment to a touch of post-celebration blues. Take the time to acknowledge and embrace these emotions, understanding that each sentiment is a brushstroke on the canvas of your shared experience.

Positive emotions may manifest in the form of sheer happiness, gratitude for the magical day, and a deep sense of fulfillment. These are the emotions that echo the vows you exchanged, the laughter that resonated through the natural landscape, and the love that enveloped you both. Bask in the warmth of these feelings, allowing them to solidify the beauty of your shared commitment.

Conversely, it's not uncommon to experience a sense of melancholy or nostalgia post-elopement. This isn't a diminishment of the joy you felt but rather a testament to the profound impact of the celebration. Recognize that it's okay to miss certain moments, the embrace of the natural setting, or the intimacy of the ceremony. These feelings, too, are part of the intricate mosaic of emotions that follow such a significant life event.

Processing emotions also involves acknowledging any unexpected surprises or challenges that may have arisen during the elopement. Whether it's dealing with unpredictable weather or navigating logistical hiccups, understanding how these moments affected you emotionally allows for a more holistic reflection on the entire experience.

One powerful way to process these emotions is through open and honest communication with your partner. Share your thoughts, express what aspects of the elopement resonated most with you, and discuss any unexpected emotions that may have surfaced. This dialogue not only strengthens your connection but also fosters a deeper understanding of each other's perspectives.

Consider engaging in activities that bring you both comfort and joy—whether it's revisiting the location of your elopement, creating a scrapbook of memories, or simply enjoying quiet moments together. These rituals become touchstones that help ground you in the reality of your shared commitment, making the emotional processing a collaborative and enriching experience.

As you navigate the landscape of post-elopement emotions, remember that the journey doesn't end with the celebration. It's an ongoing exploration of your relationship, with each emotion and memory serving as a guidepost for the chapters yet to unfold. Embrace the complexities, cherish the joys, and continue to evolve together in the wake of your beautiful outdoor elopement.

Sharing reflections as a couple

As you stand on the precipice of the post-elopement chapter, sharing reflections as a couple becomes a poignant and enriching exercise. It's an opportunity to weave the tapestry of your individual experiences into a shared narrative, deepening your connection and understanding of the profound journey you've undertaken together.

Start by setting aside a quiet moment, away from the hustle and bustle of daily life, where you and your partner can engage in thoughtful conversation. This could be a cozy evening at home, a scenic spot that holds sentimental value, or even the very location where you exchanged your vows. The idea is to create an environment conducive to open communication and introspection.

Reflect on the highs and lows of your elopement, delving into the emotional landscapes you traversed individually. Encourage each other to express what moments stood out, the unexpected joys, and any challenges faced. This dialogue allows for a deeper understanding of your partner's unique perspective and the intricate nuances that shaped their experience.

Share the details that made the day memorable for you. It could be the way the sunlight filtered through the trees during the ceremony, the sound of laughter echoing in the open air, or the feeling of being surrounded by nature's embrace. By vocalizing these moments, you not only relive them but also gift your partner a window into the kaleidoscope of your emotional world.

Equally important is discussing any unexpected emotions that may have surfaced. Whether it's the bittersweet realization that the day passed too quickly or a profound connection to the natural setting, exploring these feelings together fosters emotional intimacy. Embrace vulnerability, allowing your partner to witness the depth of your emotional experience.

Consider framing your reflections around the vows you exchanged. Reflect on how those promises manifested during the elopement and discuss how they continue to guide your journey as a couple. This provides a beautiful thread of continuity, connecting the vows spoken on your special day to the evolving narrative of your shared life.

As you share reflections, keep in mind that this isn't about finding solutions or addressing concerns—it's a celebration of your journey, a mutual acknowledgment of the beauty and complexity of your shared experience. Embrace the diversity of your reflections, understanding that each contributes to the rich tapestry of your relationship.

Ultimately, sharing reflections as a couple is an ongoing process. Just as your relationship evolves, so too will your perspectives on the elopement. Continue these conversations in the weeks and months that follow, allowing your shared reflections to become touchstones that strengthen the foundation of your enduring love story.

Integrating the Adventure into Married Life

As you transition from the elopement adventure into the everyday tapestry of married life, the challenge lies in integrating the essence of your unique journey into the fabric of your shared experiences. The memories forged during your elopement can serve as touchstones, grounding your marriage in the spirit of adventure and connection that defined your special day.

Begin by identifying elements from your elopement that encapsulate the spirit of adventure you both embraced. Whether it's the thrill of exploring a new place together, the spontaneity of your outdoor ceremony, or the shared laughter echoing through the wilderness, pinpoint those aspects that resonate most profoundly with both of you.

Consider how these elements can be woven into your daily life. Perhaps you can embark on regular outdoor escapades, fostering a sense of exploration and discovery in your marriage. This might involve weekend hikes, impromptu picnics in natural settings, or simply taking the scenic route on your way home. The goal is to infuse your routine with the same spontaneity and joy that characterized your elopement.

Look to the vows you exchanged as guiding principles for your shared life. Revisit them together and discuss how you can actively incorporate the sentiments expressed into your daily interactions. Whether it's fostering open communication, prioritizing each other's well-being, or embracing the adventure of facing life's challenges hand in hand, these vows serve as a roadmap for navigating the journey of marriage.

Integrate elements of your elopement into your home environment. This could involve incorporating natural decor reminiscent of your outdoor ceremony, displaying photographs that capture the essence of your adventure, or even planting a symbolic tree in your garden. Surrounding yourselves with tangible reminders of your elopement creates a visual and emotional connection to the shared experience.

Explore new hobbies or activities together, inspired by the interests and passions you discovered during the elopement. Whether it's taking up photography to capture more shared moments or trying your hand at adventure sports, these joint pursuits become an extension of the adventurous spirit you cultivated on your special day.

Celebrate anniversaries or milestones by revisiting the location of your elopement or embarking on similar adventures. This creates a tradition that reaffirms your commitment to keeping the flame of adventure alive in your marriage. Each return to these spaces becomes a pilgrimage, allowing you to reconnect with the magic of your elopement.

Remember, the key to integrating the adventure into married life lies in intentional, collaborative effort. By consistently infusing your relationship with the spirit of exploration, spontaneity, and shared joy, you transform your marriage into a perpetual adventure—one that evolves and deepens with each passing day. Embrace the journey, drawing inspiration from the unique love story you authored on the day you chose to elope.

Translating the spirit of the elopement into everyday life

As you embark on the journey of integrating the spirit of your elopement into your everyday life, it's essential to view this process as an ongoing narrative, a continuation of the unique love story that unfolded on your special day. Translating the spirit of the elopement into your daily existence is about infusing ordinary moments with the extraordinary sense of adventure and connection that characterized your celebration.

Start by reflecting on the core values and sentiments that defined your elopement experience. What were the key elements that made it special? Was it the intimacy, the spontaneity, the connection with nature, or a combination of these factors? Understanding these foundational aspects will guide you in translating them into your daily life.

Consider how you can infuse a sense of adventure into your routine. This doesn't necessarily mean embarking on grand voyages every day; rather, it involves approaching everyday activities with a renewed spirit. Whether it's trying new recipes together, exploring local parks, or even taking a different route during your daily walk, the goal is to inject a sense of novelty and discovery into your shared experiences.

Maintain open communication about your individual and collective goals, dreams, and aspirations. The spirit of adventure is closely tied to growth and exploration, and fostering an environment where both partners feel supported in pursuing their passions contributes to the continued narrative of your shared journey.

Create intentional moments of connection. In the midst of busy schedules, it's easy to lose sight of the importance of quality time together. Set aside regular moments for meaningful conversations, shared activities, or even quiet moments of reflection. These deliberate connections serve as threads weaving the tapestry of your ongoing love story.

Incorporate elements of nature into your daily life. If your elopement was set against a backdrop of natural beauty, bring a touch of that environment into your home. This could involve adding plants, creating a nature-inspired decor, or simply spending more time outdoors together. Connecting with nature can evoke the same sense of tranquility and wonder that characterized your elopement.

Continue the tradition of spontaneity. While routines are a part of daily life, leave room for unpredictability and surprise. Embrace spontaneous gestures, unplanned adventures, and the joy of shared surprises. This element of unpredictability keeps the flame of excitement alive in your relationship.

Regularly revisit the memories of your elopement through photographs, keepsakes, or even by revisiting the location. This reflective practice serves as a reminder of the vows and promises made on that day, reinforcing the commitment to continue the journey together.

Ultimately, translating the spirit of your elopement into everyday life is an ongoing process of co-creation. By consciously infusing your daily experiences with the essence of adventure, intimacy, and shared joy, you breathe life into the pages of your love story. Embrace the ordinary moments as opportunities to continue crafting a narrative that is uniquely yours.

Sustaining the connection with nature beyond the wedding day

Sustaining the connection with nature beyond the wedding day is an enriching journey that extends the vitality and serenity of your elopement into your daily lives. The natural world, which served as a backdrop to your celebration, can continue to be a wellspring of inspiration, tranquility, and connection for both you and your partner.

As you transition from the elopement to daily life, consider incorporating nature into your routine. Whether it's a morning walk in a nearby park, gardening together, or stargazing on clear nights, these simple rituals can be profound in grounding your connection with the natural world. Nature, with its ever-changing beauty, offers a canvas for shared moments of reflection and awe.

Bring the outdoors into your home by integrating natural elements into your living space. Houseplants, botanical artwork, or even the scent of nature-inspired candles can evoke the same sense of calm and beauty that you experienced during your elopement. These subtle reminders serve as touchpoints to the enchanting landscapes that witnessed your vows.

Plan periodic escapes to natural settings, even if they are short day trips. Whether it's revisiting the location of your elopement or exploring new natural landscapes together, these outings provide an opportunity to rejuvenate your spirits, away from the demands of daily life. The shared experiences in nature become threads woven into the fabric of your relationship.

Consider adopting sustainable practices in your lifestyle. Embracing eco-friendly choices, such as reducing waste, conserving energy, and supporting environmentally conscious products, aligns with the spirit of nature and can be a shared commitment that enhances your connection with the environment.

Engage in activities that deepen your understanding and appreciation of the natural world. Attend nature workshops, join conservation efforts, or simply immerse yourselves in educational resources about the local flora and fauna. This shared curiosity fosters a sense of shared purpose and a deeper connection with the ecosystems that surround you.

Create nature-inspired traditions. Whether it's an annual camping trip, a nature-themed date night, or seasonal rituals tied to the changing landscape, these traditions become threads that weave the connection with nature into the tapestry of your relationship. They serve as reminders of your commitment to each other and to the beauty of the world around you.

Capture and celebrate moments in nature through art, photography, or journaling. Documenting your experiences allows you to revisit and relive those cherished moments. The act of creative expression becomes a celebration of your ongoing connection with nature, preserving the visual and emotional imprints of your shared outdoor adventures.

By sustaining the connection with nature beyond the wedding day, you infuse your lives with the enduring vitality and harmony found in the natural world. It becomes a testament to the ongoing narrative of your love story—a story interwoven with the elements, landscapes, and the ever-changing beauty of the world you navigate together.

Chapter 11: Conclusion

As you embark on the final chapter of this guide, it's time to reflect on the journey you've taken toward creating a meaningful and memorable outdoor elopement. Chapter 11: Conclusion encapsulates the essence of the adventures you've explored, the love you've celebrated, and the connection you've forged with nature.

Throughout the preceding chapters, you've delved into the intricacies of planning an outdoor elopement that reflects your unique love story. From scouting picturesque locations to navigating legalities, considering the ever-changing weather to crafting an adventure-packed itinerary, each section has contributed to the tapestry of your personalized celebration.

Your journey has taken you through the seasons, exploring how nature can influence not only the backdrop of your ceremony but also the atmosphere and mood of your special day. You've discovered the beauty in embracing the elements, learned to adapt plans to regional climates, and developed flexible contingency plans for unpredictable weather.

The guide has encouraged you to weave your love story into every aspect of your elopement—from selecting attire that harmonizes with natural surroundings to personalizing vows inspired by the beauty around you. You've explored the art of capturing candid moments through photography, preserving memories beyond photographs, and ensuring that your ceremony remains intimate amid adventurous plans.

Family and friends have found their place in your elopement, and you've navigated the delicate balance between an intimate celebration and involving a wider circle. Your budget-friendly adventure has been outlined, providing tips and ideas to make your elopement not only memorable but also financially sensible.

As you conclude this guide, remember that your outdoor elopement is more than just a single day; it's a celebration of your love story that extends into the rich tapestry of your shared life. The reflections, integrations, and sustainable connections with nature discussed in the final chapters are invitations to continue the adventure long after the vows are exchanged.

Chapter 11 invites you to linger a little longer in the world you've crafted—a world filled with love, adventure, and the enduring beauty of nature. It's a celebration of the journey you've undertaken and a prelude to the countless adventures that await as you step into the next chapter of your shared story.

Recap of Key Takeaways

As you pause to reflect on the culmination of your journey through this guide, let's revisit some key takeaways that will serve as touchstones for your outdoor elopement. Throughout the chapters, you've discovered the art of crafting an intimate and adventure-packed celebration that harmonizes with nature and resonates with the unique story of your love. Here, we encapsulate the essence of those learnings.

1. Personal Preferences: The foundation of your outdoor elopement lies in understanding and reflecting on your personal preferences. Whether it's the choice of location, the style of your ceremony, or the overall atmosphere, let your unique tastes guide the decisions you make.

2. Legalities and Permits: Navigating legal requirements is a crucial step in planning your outdoor celebration. Researching and obtaining necessary permits ensures that your ceremony adheres to local regulations, allowing you to exchange vows in your chosen natural setting without hiccups.

3. Accessibility and Logistics: Evaluating accessibility for you and your guests, along with meticulous planning of logistics, guarantees a smooth and enjoyable celebration. From transportation to the venue layout, these considerations contribute to the overall comfort of everyone involved.

4. Weather Considerations: Acknowledging and embracing the elements is pivotal. From exploring the pros and cons of each season to developing flexible contingency plans, you've learned to navigate the unpredictable weather, ensuring your ceremony remains a beautiful and memorable affair.

5. Crafting an Adventure-Packed Itinerary: Pre-wedding adventures set the stage for a celebration that extends beyond the ceremony. Bonding experiences, a memorable ceremony, and post-ceremony adventures strike a balance between adventure and intimacy, creating a holistic and joyous experience.

6. Photography and Memories: Choosing the right photographer, capturing candid moments, and preserving memories go hand in hand. Collaborating with photographers to tell your unique story ensures that your outdoor elopement lives on in timeless images and cherished keepsakes.

7. Attire and Style: Your attire should not only complement the natural surroundings but also align with the casual and unconventional style you've chosen. From footwear to hair and makeup, every element contributes to the overall aesthetic of your celebration.

8. Personalizing Your Outdoor Ceremony: Incorporating nature into decor, writing personal vows, and exploring symbolic rituals infuse your ceremony with authenticity and emotional depth. These personalized elements make your celebration a true reflection of your love story.

9. Family and Friends: Communicating your choice to elope, involving loved ones, and celebrating with a wider circle have been delicate yet essential considerations. Balancing intimacy with broader social connections ensures that your closest relationships play a meaningful role in your celebration.

10. Budget-Friendly Outdoor Elopements: From cost-saving strategies to DIY decor and affordable adventure options, you've learned to navigate the financial aspects of your celebration without compromising its richness. Eloping on a budget is not just practical; it's an opportunity to infuse creativity and personal touches into every detail.

11. Post-Elopement Reflection and Integration: The journey doesn't end with the ceremony. Reflecting on the experience, sharing reflections as a couple, and integrating the adventure into married life are steps that ensure your elopement continues to shape your shared narrative long after the vows are exchanged.

In essence, your outdoor elopement is a canvas upon which you paint your unique love story. By embracing nature, crafting an adventure, personalizing every detail, and involving your nearest and dearest, you've created a celebration that goes beyond tradition—a celebration that reflects the authenticity of your love. As you move forward, remember that the memories and experiences you've curated will forever be etched in the tapestry of your shared journey.